I0004292

Mastering Adobe Creative Cloud with Quiz

Table of Contents

Chapter 1: Introduction to Adobe Creative Cloud

Introduction to Adobe Creative Cloud:

Adobe Creative Cloud (CC) is a comprehensive suite of software applications and services developed by Adobe Systems. It provides a wide range of creative tools for various digital media needs, including graphic design, video editing, photography, web development, and more. Unlike Adobe's traditional software model, where users purchased and owned individual software licenses, Creative Cloud operates on a subscription-based model. This means users pay a monthly or annual fee to access the entire suite of Adobe applications and services.

Understanding the Concept of Creative Cloud:

Subscription Model:

Creative Cloud's subscription model allows users to access Adobe's software applications and services through a monthly or annual subscription plan. This approach has several benefits:

Affordability: Subscriptions are often more affordable upfront compared to purchasing individual licenses for each software separately.

Constant Updates: Subscribers receive regular updates and new features as part of their subscription, ensuring they always have access to the latest tools and improvements.

Flexibility: Users can choose different subscription plans based on their needs, whether they're individuals, businesses, or students.

Cloud-Based Services:

The term "Creative Cloud" implies the integration of cloud-based services into Adobe's software ecosystem. This includes services like cloud storage, file sharing, collaboration, and asset management. Some key aspects include:

Cloud Storage: Users are provided with cloud storage space where they can store and access their work files from any device with an internet connection.

File Syncing: Files stored in the Creative Cloud are automatically synced across devices, ensuring consistency and accessibility.

Collaboration: Creative Cloud enables real-time collaboration, allowing multiple users to work on the same project simultaneously from different locations.

Asset Libraries: Users can store frequently used assets such as images, logos, and templates in cloud-based libraries, making them easily accessible across Adobe applications.

Application Variety:

Adobe Creative Cloud includes a wide array of software applications, catering to different creative needs. Some of the notable applications include:

Photoshop: A powerful image editing and manipulation tool.

Illustrator: Used for vector graphic design and illustration.

InDesign: Primarily for desktop publishing and layout design.

Premiere Pro: For professional video editing and production.

After Effects: Used for motion graphics and visual effects in videos.

Lightroom: Designed for photo editing and organization.

XD: A tool for user experience and user interface design.

Cross-Application Integration:

One of the strengths of Creative Cloud is the seamless integration between its applications. This integration allows users to move assets and projects between different applications with ease, enhancing workflow efficiency and creativity.

Mobile Apps and Accessibility:

Adobe has developed mobile versions of many Creative Cloud applications, making it possible for users to work on their projects using smartphones and tablets. This accessibility promotes creative freedom by allowing users to capture ideas and make edits on the go.

Learning Resources:

Creative Cloud provides access to a plethora of learning resources, including tutorials, guides, and templates. This assists both beginners and experienced users in mastering the applications and techniques.

Conclusion:

Adobe Creative Cloud revolutionized the creative software industry by introducing a subscription-based model, cloud-based services, cross-application integration, and accessibility. The concept of Creative Cloud empowers individuals and teams to create, collaborate, and innovate across a diverse range of creative fields, making it a cornerstone in modern digital creativity.

QUIZ

Question 1: What is the primary advantage of Adobe Creative Cloud's subscription model?

a) Access to a single software application

b) One-time purchase of software licenses

c) Regular updates and new features

d) No need for an internet connection

Answer: c) Regular updates and new features

Question 2: What is the purpose of cloud storage in Adobe Creative Cloud?

a) To provide virtual reality experiences

b) To host online gaming servers

c) To store and access work files from any device

d) To render 3D animations

Answer: c) To store and access work files from any device

Question 3: Which Adobe application is primarily used for vector graphic design and illustration?

a) Photoshop

b) Premiere Pro

c) Illustrator

d) After Effects

Answer: c) Illustrator

Question 4: How does Adobe Creative Cloud promote collaboration among users?

a) By restricting file access to a single user at a time

b) By allowing real-time collaboration on the same project

c) By limiting the number of users who can access a project

d) By making collaboration only possible in-person

Answer: b) By allowing real-time collaboration on the same project

Question 5: What is the benefit of using cloud-based libraries in Adobe Creative Cloud?

a) They allow users to play online games

b) They enable users to share their files publicly

c) They store frequently used assets for easy access

d) They automatically update software applications

Answer: c) They store frequently used assets for easy access

Question 6: Which Adobe application is specifically designed for user experience and user interface design?

a) InDesign

b) Lightroom

c) XD

d) After Effects

Answer: c) XD

Question 7: How does Adobe Creative Cloud enhance accessibility for users?

a) By limiting access to only one device

b) By requiring a high-speed internet connection

c) By providing mobile versions of applications

d) By excluding users without technical skills

Answer: c) By providing mobile versions of applications

Overview of Adobe's software suite

Introduction to Adobe's Software Suite:

Adobe's software suite, available through Adobe Creative Cloud, offers a diverse range of applications catering to various creative needs. Each application is specialized for specific tasks, from graphic design and video editing to photography and web development. These applications are widely used by professionals and enthusiasts in industries such as design, media, marketing, and more. In this overview, we'll explore some key applications within Adobe's software suite.

1. Photoshop:

Adobe Photoshop is a flagship application for image editing, manipulation, and creation. It offers a plethora of tools and features for retouching photos, creating digital art, and designing graphics. Photoshop's capabilities include layers, filters, brushes, and extensive color correction tools.

2. Illustrator:

Adobe Illustrator is a vector graphic design application. It's used for creating logos, icons, illustrations, and other scalable graphics. Illustrator's unique feature is its ability to create images based on mathematical equations, ensuring crisp quality at any size.

3. InDesign:

Adobe InDesign is a desktop publishing application tailored for creating layouts for print and digital publications. It's used for designing magazines, brochures, books, and interactive PDFs, offering advanced typography and layout tools.

4. Premiere Pro:

Adobe Premiere Pro is a professional video editing application. It's widely used for video production, offering features like timeline editing, color correction, audio editing, and seamless integration with other Adobe applications.

5. After Effects:

Adobe After Effects specializes in motion graphics, visual effects, and compositing for videos. It's used to create animations, title sequences, and complex visual effects. After Effects' timeline-based interface is essential for creating dynamic animations.

6. Lightroom:

Adobe Lightroom is designed for photo editing and organization. It provides non-destructive editing tools, batch processing, and advanced color correction. Lightroom is popular among photographers for its ability to manage large collections of photos.

7. Adobe XD:

Adobe XD is a user experience (UX) and user interface (UI) design application. It's used for creating interactive prototypes, wireframes, and designs for websites and mobile apps. XD streamlines the design and collaboration process.

8. Dreamweaver:

Adobe Dreamweaver is an application for web development and design. It offers both visual and code-based approaches for creating websites and web applications. Dreamweaver's integration with other Adobe tools simplifies asset management.

9. Audition:

Adobe Audition is an audio editing application. It's used for recording, mixing, and editing audio tracks for various purposes, including podcasts, music production, and video soundtracks.

10. Animate:

Adobe Animate is used for creating interactive animations and multimedia content. It's often used to design web banners, animated characters, and interactive web elements.

Conclusion:

Adobe's software suite, available through Creative Cloud, encompasses a wide range of specialized applications that empower creative professionals and enthusiasts to bring their ideas to life. These applications offer powerful tools for image editing, graphic design, video production, web development, and more. Understanding each application's purpose and capabilities is essential for effectively utilizing the resources provided by Adobe Creative Cloud.

QUIZ

Question 1: Which Adobe application is primarily used for image editing, manipulation, and digital art creation?

a) Illustrator

b) InDesign

c) Premiere Pro

d) Photoshop

Answer: d) Photoshop

Question 2: What type of graphics is Adobe Illustrator best suited for creating?

a) Animated graphics

b) Vector graphics

c) 3D graphics

d) Pixel graphics

Answer: b) Vector graphics

Question 3: Which Adobe application is used for designing layouts for print and digital publications, such as magazines and brochures?

a) Illustrator

b) InDesign

c) Photoshop

d) Premiere Pro

Answer: b) InDesign

Question 4: What is the main purpose of Adobe Premiere Pro?

a) Photo editing

b) Vector illustration

c) Video editing and production

d) 3D animation

Answer: c) Video editing and production

Question 5: Which Adobe application is used for creating motion graphics, visual effects, and compositing in videos?

a) After Effects

b) Lightroom

c) Illustrator

d) Audition

Answer: a) After Effects

Question 6: Adobe Lightroom is primarily used for:

a) Video editing

b) Web development

c) Photo editing and organization

d) Vector illustration

Answer: c) Photo editing and organization

Question 7: Which Adobe application is specifically designed for user experience (UX) and user interface (UI) design?

a) InDesign

b) Premiere Pro

c) Animate

d) Adobe XD

Answer: d) Adobe XD

Chapter 2: Getting Started with Adobe Account

Creating and managing an Adobe ID

In today's digital age, Adobe offers a wide range of creative and productivity tools that cater to professionals, artists, designers, photographers, and various other creative enthusiasts. To access and utilize these tools effectively, users are required to create an Adobe ID. An Adobe ID serves as a universal key to unlock Adobe's suite of software, services, and resources. This chapter delves into the process of creating and managing an Adobe ID, which is a crucial initial step in your Adobe journey.

Creating an Adobe ID:

Accessing the Adobe Website: To start the process of creating an Adobe ID, you need to visit the official Adobe website (www.adobe.com).

Sign Up/Log In: On the Adobe website, you'll typically find a "Sign In" or "Start for Free" option, depending on whether you already have an Adobe ID or not. If you're new to Adobe, select the "Start for Free" option to initiate the sign-up process.

Personal Information: During the sign-up process, Adobe will prompt you to provide your personal information, including your first name, last name, email address, and password. Ensure that you choose a strong password to enhance the security of your Adobe ID.

Verification: After providing your email address, Adobe may send you a verification email. Access your email inbox, locate the verification email from Adobe, and click on the verification link. This step confirms that the provided email address is valid and associated with you.

Profile Information: Once your email is verified, you'll be directed to a page where you can provide additional profile information. This might include your country of residence, your role (professional, student, hobbyist, etc.), and your interests. Filling out this information can help tailor your Adobe experience to your preferences.

Agree to Terms: Like most online services, Adobe has terms of use and privacy policies. Read through these documents carefully and agree to them if you're comfortable with the terms.

Adobe ID Creation: With all the required information provided and agreements in place, you can finalize the creation of your Adobe ID. This ID is linked to your email address and password and will be used to log in to Adobe services and products.

Managing Your Adobe ID:

Logging In: Once your Adobe ID is created, you can log in to Adobe services using your registered email address and password. This will give you access to Adobe's software, cloud services, and community forums.

Security Settings: To enhance the security of your Adobe ID, consider enabling two-factor authentication (2FA). This adds an extra layer of protection by requiring a verification code from your mobile device when logging in.

Profile Management: You can manage your profile information, such as updating your name, email address, and preferences, by accessing the account settings on the Adobe website. Keeping your profile up to date ensures that Adobe can communicate with you effectively.

Subscription Management: If you have subscribed to Adobe's Creative Cloud or other services, you can manage your subscriptions through your Adobe account. This includes upgrading, downgrading, or canceling subscriptions.

Password Management: Regularly update your password to maintain the security of your Adobe ID. If you forget your password, there are options to reset it using your registered email address.

Connected Devices: Adobe may allow you to activate its software on a certain number of devices based on your subscription. You can manage these activations through your Adobe account to ensure that you're using the software on the devices you want.

Conclusion:

Creating and managing an Adobe ID is an essential step to access and utilize Adobe's wide array of creative tools and services. By carefully setting up your Adobe ID, securing it with strong passwords and 2FA, and managing your profile, subscriptions, and settings, you can enjoy a seamless and secure Adobe experience tailored to your creative needs.

QUIZ

Question 1: What is the primary purpose of an Adobe ID?

A) Accessing Adobe's official website

B) Creating documents in Adobe Illustrator

C) Logging into Adobe services and products

D) Managing email subscriptions

Answer: C) Logging into Adobe services and products

Question 2: During the sign-up process for an Adobe ID, what is the purpose of email verification?

A) To confirm your mailing address

B) To send you promotional offers

C) To verify the validity of the provided email address

D) To set up two-factor authentication

Answer: C) To verify the validity of the provided email address

Question 3: Which of the following can you manage through your Adobe account settings?

A) Your social media accounts

B) Your personal blog

C) Your subscription to a local newspaper

D) Your profile information and preferences

Answer: D) Your profile information and preferences

Question 4: What should you consider when choosing a password for your Adobe ID?

A) Using a password you've used for other accounts

B) Creating a password with your name and birthdate

C) Choosing a strong and unique password

D) Selecting a password that's easy to guess

Answer: C) Choosing a strong and unique password

Question 5: What is two-factor authentication (2FA) and why is it important for your Adobe ID?

A) It's a feature that automatically logs you out of Adobe services

B) It's a way to access Adobe products without a password

C) It's a security measure that adds an extra layer of protection by requiring a verification code

D) It's a feature that connects your Adobe ID to your social media accounts

Answer: C) It's a security measure that adds an extra layer of protection by requiring a verification code

Question 6: How can you manage your subscriptions to Adobe services through your Adobe ID?

A) By sending an email to Adobe's customer support

B) By uninstalling Adobe software from your devices

C) By contacting your internet service provider

D) By accessing your Adobe account settings

Answer: D) By accessing your Adobe account settings

Question 7: What information might you provide in your Adobe profile to tailor your experience?

A) Your favorite color

B) Your favorite movie

C) Your country of residence and role

D) Your favorite food

Answer: C) Your country of residence and role

Subscribing to Creative Cloud plans

Choose a Plan: Visit the official Adobe website and navigate to the Creative Cloud section. Here, you will find a variety of subscription plans tailored to different needs. These plans might include options for individuals, students, businesses, and photographers. Carefully review the features and software included in each plan to determine which best suits your requirements.

Sign In or Sign Up: If you already have an Adobe ID, sign in using your credentials. If not, you'll need to create an Adobe ID as discussed in Chapter 2. This ID will serve as the foundation for managing your Creative Cloud subscription.

Select a Plan Tier: Within each subscription plan, there are often different tiers with varying levels of features and software access. Choose the tier that aligns with your creative needs and budget. For instance, some plans might provide access to just a single application, while others offer access to the entire suite.

Billing Information: Provide your billing information, including credit card details or other preferred payment methods. Adobe generally offers monthly and annual payment options, and the price may vary based on the plan and tier you choose.

Confirm Subscription: Review your subscription details, including the plan, tier, and billing information, to ensure accuracy. Once you're satisfied, confirm your subscription. Adobe will usually provide an overview of the payment schedule and any applicable taxes.

Download and Install Software: After successfully subscribing, you can access your Creative Cloud account dashboard. From there, you can download and install the software applications included in your chosen plan. Adobe offers a desktop application called the Creative Cloud Desktop app, which serves as a hub for managing your installed applications, updates, and more.

Cloud Services and Storage: Many Creative Cloud plans include cloud-based services, such as Adobe Stock for accessing high-quality images, fonts, and graphics, or Adobe Spark for creating web pages and social media posts. You may also get access to cloud storage, allowing you to save and synchronize your work across different devices.

Managing Your Subscription: Your Creative Cloud subscription can be managed through your Adobe account settings. This includes options to upgrade or downgrade your plan, cancel your subscription, or change payment methods. Regularly review your subscription to ensure it aligns with your evolving creative needs.

Benefits of Creative Cloud Subscription:

Access to Latest Software: Subscribing to Creative Cloud provides you with the latest versions of Adobe's software applications, ensuring you have access to the most up-to-date features and enhancements.

Regular Updates: Adobe frequently releases updates to its software, addressing bugs, adding new features, and improving performance. Subscribers receive these updates automatically as part of their subscription.

Cloud Integration: Creative Cloud applications are integrated with Adobe's cloud services, allowing for easy collaboration, sharing, and syncing of projects across devices.

Access to Adobe Fonts: Many Creative Cloud plans include access to Adobe Fonts (formerly Typekit), providing a vast library of fonts for your design projects.

Adobe Stock Integration: Depending on your plan, you might get access to Adobe Stock, a vast collection of images, videos, and graphics that can enhance your creative projects.

Conclusion:

Subscribing to Creative Cloud plans opens the door to a world of creative possibilities, enabling you to access, explore, and utilize Adobe's powerful software suite along with its cloud-based services. By carefully selecting the right plan, managing your subscription through your Adobe account settings, and leveraging the benefits of cloud integration, you can take your creative endeavors to new heights.

QUIZ

Question 1: What is the primary purpose of subscribing to Adobe Creative Cloud plans?

A) Accessing social media accounts

B) Playing online games

C) Using email services

D) Gaining access to Adobe's suite of software and services

Answer: D) Gaining access to Adobe's suite of software and services

Question 2: How can you access different subscription plans for Adobe Creative Cloud?

A) Through physical retail stores only

B) By contacting Adobe's customer support

C) By visiting the official Adobe website

D) By sending an email request

Answer: C) By visiting the official Adobe website

Question 3: Which of the following is NOT typically included in a Creative Cloud subscription plan?

A) Access to cloud storage

B) Adobe Stock images and videos

C) Microsoft Office Suite

D) Regular software updates

Answer: C) Microsoft Office Suite

Question 4: What is the purpose of the Creative Cloud Desktop app?

A) To create and edit documents

B) To manage your subscription payment

C) To provide access to cloud storage

D) To manage installed applications, updates, and more

Answer: D) To manage installed applications, updates, and more

Question 5: What is one benefit of subscribing to Creative Cloud in terms of software updates?

A) You need to manually search for updates

B) Updates are not available for subscribers

C) You receive automatic updates with the latest features

D) Updates require an additional fee

Answer: C) You receive automatic updates with the latest features

Question 6: How can you manage your Creative Cloud subscription?

A) Through a local retail store

B) By calling Adobe's customer service hotline

C) By accessing your Adobe account settings

D) By uninstalling Creative Cloud applications

Answer: C) By accessing your Adobe account settings

Question 7: What type of content might be available through Adobe Stock, depending on your subscription plan?

A) Recipes for cooking

B) Videos of cute animals

C) High-quality images, videos, and graphics

D) Free access to music

Answer: C) High-quality images, videos, and graphics

Chapter 3: Adobe Photoshop Essentials

Introduction to Photoshop and its capabilities

Adobe Photoshop is a powerful and versatile raster graphics editing software developed by Adobe Inc. It is a staple tool in the field of digital design, photography, and image manipulation. With a wide range of tools and features, Photoshop allows users to create, edit, and enhance images to achieve stunning visual results.

Capabilities of Adobe Photoshop:

Image Editing: Photoshop is renowned for its unparalleled image editing capabilities. It allows users to manipulate various aspects of an image, such as color, exposure, contrast, and sharpness. This makes it an indispensable tool for photographers and designers who need to retouch and refine their images.

Layers and Masks: One of the most powerful features of Photoshop is its ability to work with layers. Layers allow users to stack different elements of an image separately, enabling precise editing without affecting the rest of the composition. Layer masks provide even more control by allowing selective adjustments, enabling users to hide or reveal specific parts of a layer.

Selection Tools: Photoshop provides an array of selection tools that allow users to isolate specific areas of an image for editing. From simple rectangular or elliptical selections to more complex tools like the Magic Wand and Quick Selection tool, users can make precise edits to specific regions.

Retouching and Healing: The software offers tools like the Clone Stamp, Healing Brush, and Content-Aware Fill to remove blemishes, wrinkles, and unwanted objects from images seamlessly. These tools make it possible to achieve flawless results in portrait and product photography.

Text and Typography: Photoshop isn't just about working with images; it also offers robust text and typography tools. Users can add, format, and manipulate text within their designs, incorporating creative typography to convey messages effectively.

Filters and Effects: Photoshop provides an extensive library of filters and effects that can transform images in various ways. Users can apply artistic effects, simulate different types of media (like pencil sketches or watercolors), and enhance images with lighting and texture effects.

Drawing and Painting: For artists and illustrators, Photoshop offers a range of brushes and drawing tools that simulate traditional art mediums. With pressure sensitivity and customizable brush settings, users can create intricate digital paintings and illustrations.

Color Correction and Grading: Photoshop excels in color correction and grading. Users can adjust color balance, hue, saturation, and luminance to achieve desired color effects. This is crucial for creating a consistent look across a series of images.

3D and Motion Graphics: Photoshop supports 3D modeling and texturing, allowing users to create 3D objects and scenes. It's also possible to create simple animations and video editing within the software.

Web and UI Design: Photoshop is a valuable tool for web and user interface (UI) designers. It offers tools to design website layouts, create buttons, icons, and other UI elements, and then export them in web-friendly formats.

Batch Processing: Photoshop includes automation tools that enable users to apply the same edits to multiple images simultaneously, saving time and maintaining consistency.

Conclusion:

Adobe Photoshop is a multifaceted software that serves as the cornerstone of digital design and image editing. In Chapter 3 of Adobe Photoshop Essentials, the software's essential capabilities are explored, providing users with a solid foundation to harness its potential for creative and professional endeavors. From basic image adjustments to advanced retouching and 3D modeling, Photoshop remains an indispensable tool for visual artists across various industries.

QUIZ

Question 1: What is the primary purpose of Adobe Photoshop?

a) Video editing

b) 3D modeling

c) Vector illustration

d) Image editing

Answer: d) Image editing

Question 2: Which feature in Photoshop allows you to edit different parts of an image without affecting the rest?

a) Layers

b) Filters

c) Brushes

d) Selection tools

Answer: a) Layers

Question 3: Which tool is used to remove blemishes, wrinkles, and unwanted objects from images?

a) Pen Tool

b) Magic Wand

c) Clone Stamp

d) Gradient Tool

Answer: c) Clone Stamp

Question 4: What is the purpose of layer masks in Photoshop?

a) Adding text to an image

b) Applying filters to an image

c) Isolating specific parts of a layer for selective editing

d) Creating 3D objects

Answer: c) Isolating specific parts of a layer for selective editing

Question 5: Which tool allows you to make precise selections of specific areas in an image?

a) Crop Tool

b) Brush Tool

c) Lasso Tool

d) Move Tool

Answer: c) Lasso Tool

Question 6: What is the primary function of the Content-Aware Fill tool in Photoshop?

a) Adjusting image exposure

b) Applying artistic filters

c) Removing unwanted objects from images

d) Adding text to images

Answer: c) Removing unwanted objects from images

Question 7: What can Photoshop's 3D capabilities be used for?

a) Creating complex vector illustrations

b) Simulating traditional painting techniques

c) Editing video footage

d) Designing 3D objects and scenes

Answer: d) Designing 3D objects and scenes

Basic image editing and manipulation

Crop and Resize:

The crop tool allows users to remove unwanted portions of an image and focus on the subject. This is useful for improving composition and eliminating distractions. The resize function helps adjust the dimensions of an image, important for preparing images for different purposes, such as web or print.

Brightness and Contrast Adjustment:

Adjusting brightness and contrast can dramatically improve the overall appearance of an image. Photoshop provides tools like "Brightness/Contrast" and "Levels" that allow users to control the luminance and contrast levels of an image.

Color Correction:

Photoshop's color correction tools enable users to adjust color balance, hue, saturation, and vibrancy. This is particularly useful for correcting color casts in images and achieving consistent color across a series of photos.

Sharpening and Blurring:

The "Sharpen" tool enhances the sharpness and clarity of details in an image, while the "Blur" tool can be used to create artistic effects or simulate shallow depth of field.

Selections and Masking:

Selection tools allow users to isolate specific parts of an image for editing. This is particularly useful when you want to apply edits to only certain areas. Layer masks further refine this by allowing selective editing on specific layers.

Healing and Spot Removal:

The "Healing Brush" and "Spot Healing Brush" tools help remove blemishes, wrinkles, and unwanted objects from images seamlessly. These tools sample nearby pixels to replace imperfections with more appropriate content.

Adjustment Layers:

Adjustment layers are non-destructive tools that allow users to apply various adjustments like brightness, contrast, saturation, and more. These adjustments can be modified or removed at any time without affecting the original image.

Filters and Effects:

Photoshop offers a wide range of filters and effects that can be applied to images to create various artistic and stylistic results. Filters include blurring, sharpening, distortions, and more.

Adding Text and Watermarks:

Users can add text to images using the text tool, allowing for captions, titles, or other textual elements. Additionally, watermarks can be added to protect images from unauthorized use.

Conclusion:

Basic image editing and manipulation are fundamental skills for anyone working with digital images, whether in photography, graphic design, or other creative fields. Chapter 3 of Adobe Photoshop Essentials covers these essential techniques in detail, equipping users with the knowledge and tools to transform their images, improve their visual impact, and set the stage for more advanced editing and creative endeavors using Adobe Photoshop.

QUIZ

Question 1: What does the crop tool in Photoshop allow you to do?

a) Adjust the brightness of an image

b) Remove unwanted portions of an image

c) Apply artistic filters to an image

d) Add text to an image

Answer: b) Remove unwanted portions of an image

Question 2: Which Photoshop tool is used to enhance the sharpness and clarity of details in an image?

a) Blur Tool

b) Eraser Tool

c) Smudge Tool

d) Sharpen Tool

Answer: d) Sharpen Tool

Question 3: What is the purpose of using layer masks in Photoshop?

a) To crop and resize images

b) To adjust color balance

c) To apply artistic filters

d) To selectively edit parts of an image

Answer: d) To selectively edit parts of an image

Question 4: Which type of layer in Photoshop allows you to apply adjustments without permanently affecting the original image?

a) Background Layer

b) Text Layer

c) Adjustment Layer

d) Smart Layer

Answer: c) Adjustment Layer

Question 5: What does the Healing Brush tool in Photoshop help you achieve?

a) Adding shadows to an image

b) Adding text to an image

c) Removing imperfections from an image

d) Applying gradients to an image

Answer: c) Removing imperfections from an image

Question 6: Which tool in Photoshop is used to adjust the balance of colors, hue, and saturation in an image?

a) Brush Tool

b) Crop Tool

c) Color Picker Tool

d) Hue/Saturation Adjustment Tool

Answer: d) Hue/Saturation Adjustment Tool

Question 7: What is the purpose of applying filters to an image in Photoshop?

a) To add text and captions to an image

b) To remove unwanted objects from an image

c) To enhance or modify the appearance of an image

d) To resize and crop an image

Answer: c) To enhance or modify the appearance of an image

Chapter 4: Advanced Photoshop Techniques

Layer management and blending modes

In the world of digital image editing and manipulation, Adobe Photoshop stands as a powerful tool that offers a wide array of features for both novice and professional users. As users progress beyond the basics, they delve into more advanced techniques, among which layer management and blending modes play a pivotal role.

Layer Management:

Understanding Layers:

Layers are the foundation of non-destructive editing in Photoshop. Each layer can contain different elements, such as images, text, shapes, adjustments, and more. They allow users to work on individual components of an image separately, making it easier to control and modify specific parts without affecting the entire composition.

Layer Organization:

Advanced Photoshop users learn the importance of organizing layers efficiently. This involves practices like grouping related layers, using folders, and appropriately naming layers to ensure clarity and ease of navigation within complex projects. Proper organization becomes crucial when dealing with intricate compositions involving numerous elements.

Layer Blending Modes:

Layer blending modes are a set of options that determine how pixels on one layer interact with pixels on underlying layers. Blending modes influence how colors, tones, and textures combine, resulting in a wide range of visual effects.

Blending Modes:

Normal Mode:

The default blending mode, where pixels on the active layer cover those on the layers beneath without any interaction.

Darkening Blending Modes:

Multiply: Multiplies the pixel values of the active layer with the values of the layers below. Darker areas become more pronounced, and lighter areas become transparent.

Linear Burn: Darkens the image while preserving the highlights. It intensifies contrast and saturation.

Lightening Blending Modes:

Screen: Opposite of Multiply. Lightens the image by brightening the areas where pixels interact.

Linear Dodge (Add): Adds the pixel values of the active layer to those below. It enhances highlights.

Contrast Blending Modes:

Overlay: Combines Multiply and Screen modes. It boosts contrast and enhances both highlights and shadows.

Soft Light: Gentle blending that adds soft highlights and shadows for a subtle, diffused effect.

Inversion Blending Modes:

Difference: Compares pixel values and subtracts underlying layer values from the active layer. Creates an inverted, high-contrast effect.

Exclusion: Similar to Difference but with a milder impact. Often used for creative and artistic effects.

Composite Blending Modes:

Hue: Applies the hue of the active layer to the underlying layers while retaining their brightness and saturation.

Saturation: Applies the saturation of the active layer to the underlying layers, preserving their hue and brightness.

Color: Blends the hue and saturation of the active layer with the luminosity of the underlying layers.

Special Effects Blending Modes:

Hard Light: Similar to Overlay but with a more pronounced effect. It intensifies highlights and shadows.

Vivid Light: Intensifies colors and contrast, producing vibrant and striking results.

Blending Modes for Text and Vector Shapes:

When working with text or vector shapes, blending modes can be applied to achieve creative text effects or merge vector shapes seamlessly with the underlying imagery.

Practical Applications:

Photo Retouching: Blending modes are used to adjust skin tones, remove blemishes, and enhance details while maintaining natural textures.

Composite Images: Layer management and blending modes are essential for combining multiple images to create surreal or harmonious compositions.

Special Effects: Advanced users can use blending modes to create lighting effects, add realistic shadows, or simulate fog and mist.

Typography and Graphic Design: Blending modes help integrate text and design elements cohesively into an image, making them appear as part of the scene.

Conclusion:

Layer management and blending modes are advanced techniques that elevate Photoshop usage beyond basic editing. They empower users to create intricate and captivating compositions, manipulate images with finesse, and achieve artistic visions that were once considered challenging. In Chapter 4 of an advanced Photoshop techniques guide, readers would gain a deeper understanding of these concepts and their applications, enabling them to take their image editing skills to new heights.

QUIZ

Question 1: What is the primary purpose of using layers in Photoshop?

A) To apply global adjustments to the entire image.

B) To merge multiple images into a single layer.

C) To work on individual elements separately and non-destructively.

D) To add special effects directly to the background layer.

Answer: C) To work on individual elements separately and non-destructively.

Question 2: Which blending mode is commonly used to darken an image and enhance contrast?

A) Screen

B) Overlay

C) Multiply

D) Color

Answer: C) Multiply

Question 3: What does the "Screen" blending mode do?

A) Darkens the image and enhances shadows.

B) Combines the hue and saturation of the active layer with the luminosity of the underlying layers.

C) Lightens the image by brightening areas where pixels interact.

D) Blends the pixel values of the active layer with those of the layers below.

Answer: C) Lightens the image by brightening areas where pixels interact.

Question 4: Which blending mode is often used to intensify both highlights and shadows in an image?

A) Overlay

B) Soft Light

C) Difference

D) Hue

Answer: A) Overlay

Question 5: What does the "Difference" blending mode do?

A) Adds the pixel values of the active layer to those below.

B) Inverts the colors of the active layer.

C) Compares pixel values and subtracts underlying layer values from the active layer.

D) Combines the hue and saturation of the active layer with the luminosity of the underlying layers.

Answer: C) Compares pixel values and subtracts underlying layer values from the active layer.

Question 6: Which blending mode applies the hue of the active layer to the underlying layers while preserving their brightness and saturation?

A) Exclusion

B) Hue

C) Color

D) Soft Light

Answer: B) Hue

Question 7: How can blending modes be applied to text and vector shapes?

A) Blending modes cannot be applied to text or vector shapes.

B) Blending modes can only be applied to vector shapes, not text.

C) By adjusting the layer opacity of text or vector shapes.

D) By changing the blending mode of the text or vector shape layer.

Answer: D) By changing the blending mode of the text or vector shape layer.

Photo retouching and restoration

In the realm of digital image editing, photo retouching and restoration are advanced techniques that require a comprehensive understanding of Adobe Photoshop's tools and functionalities. Chapter 4 of an advanced Photoshop guide often delves into these topics, offering insights and methods to transform aged or flawed photographs into visually pleasing and historically significant works of art.

Photo Retouching:

Understanding Photo Retouching:

Photo retouching involves enhancing and improving the visual quality of a photograph. This process can range from simple adjustments like color correction and exposure balancing to more intricate techniques like removing blemishes, wrinkles, or unwanted elements from the image.

Non-Destructive Editing:

Advanced Photoshop users are introduced to the concept of non-destructive editing, which allows them to make changes without permanently altering the original image. This is achieved through the use of adjustment layers, layer masks, and smart objects, ensuring that the original image data remains intact.

Tools and Techniques:

Advanced retouching often involves the use of various tools like the Clone Stamp, Healing Brush, and Content-Aware Fill. These tools enable users to seamlessly remove imperfections, reconstruct missing parts, and blend textures for a flawless result.

Frequency Separation:

Frequency separation is an advanced technique that separates the image into high and low-frequency layers. The high-frequency layer contains fine details like textures and blemishes, while the low-frequency layer holds the broader color and tone information. This allows retouchers to work on different aspects independently, enhancing the overall look without compromising details.

Photo Restoration:

Understanding Photo Restoration:

Photo restoration is the process of bringing new life to old or damaged photographs. This involves repairing torn or faded images, restoring missing parts, and improving the overall quality while maintaining the original appearance.

Digital Reconstruction:

Advanced Photoshop users are introduced to the art of digital reconstruction, where missing parts of a photograph are meticulously recreated based on existing information and historical context. This could involve rebuilding faces, objects, or backgrounds using a combination of cloning, painting, and texture blending.

Colorization:

Colorization is another aspect of photo restoration that involves adding color to black and white or faded images. Advanced techniques include using blending modes and adjustment layers to achieve natural and accurate color results.

Preserving Historical Accuracy:

Advanced Photoshop users must balance the desire to enhance the image's visual quality with the need to preserve its historical accuracy. This involves research to ensure that colors, textures, and details are consistent with the time period and context of the photograph.

Practical Applications:

Portrait Retouching: Advanced techniques allow retouchers to achieve professional-level retouching for portrait photographs, removing imperfections while maintaining a natural look.

Photo Colorization: Skilled users can breathe new life into historical images, adding color to recreate the past with authenticity.

Documenting History: Photo restoration ensures that valuable historical images are preserved for future generations, maintaining their significance and visual appeal.

Artistic Interpretation: Advanced Photoshop users can use retouching and restoration techniques to reinterpret photographs, creating unique and imaginative artworks.

Conclusion:

Chapter 4 of an advanced Photoshop techniques guide explores the art of photo retouching and restoration, offering users the tools and knowledge needed to transform ordinary or damaged images into extraordinary pieces of visual history. From removing imperfections to reconstructing missing parts, these techniques empower users to unlock the full potential of their photographs, making them more vibrant, relevant, and impactful.

QUIZ

Question 1: What is the primary goal of photo retouching in Photoshop?

A) To completely change the original image.

B) To enhance the visual quality of a photograph.

C) To replace the original image with a new one.

D) To resize the image without losing quality.

Answer: B) To enhance the visual quality of a photograph.

Question 2: Which technique separates an image into high and low-frequency layers to retouch fine details while preserving broader tones and colors?

A) Colorization

B) Frequency Separation

C) Digital Reconstruction

D) Non-Destructive Editing

Answer: B) Frequency Separation

Question 3: What is non-destructive editing in the context of photo retouching?

A) Editing the photo in a way that destroys the original image data.

B) Editing the photo without using any tools.

C) Editing the photo while keeping the original image intact.

D) Editing the photo in a way that completely changes its content.

Answer: C) Editing the photo while keeping the original image intact.

Question 4: What is the purpose of photo restoration in Photoshop?

A) To make the photo look completely different from the original.

B) To change the historical context of the photo.

C) To repair old or damaged photographs while preserving their original appearance.

D) To add artificial elements to the photo.

Answer: C) To repair old or damaged photographs while preserving their original appearance.

Question 5: What is one of the advanced techniques used in photo restoration to recreate missing parts of an image?

A) Adding random colors to the image.

B) Reducing the image's resolution.

C) Applying filters to the entire image.

D) Digital reconstruction based on existing information.

Answer: D) Digital reconstruction based on existing information.

Question 6: Which aspect of photo restoration involves adding color to black and white or faded images?

A) Frequency Separation

B) Digital Reconstruction

C) Non-Destructive Editing

D) Colorization

Answer: D) Colorization

Question 7: Why is it important to preserve historical accuracy during the photo restoration process?

A) It allows for creative interpretation of the image.

B) It helps to completely transform the image's meaning.

C) It ensures that the image's context and details are consistent with its time period.

D) It is not important; the goal is to make the image visually appealing.

Answer: C) It ensures that the image's context and details are consistent with its time period.

Chapter 5: Exploring Adobe Illustrator

Fundamentals of vector graphics

Introduction to Vector Graphics:

Vector graphics are a fundamental concept in the world of digital design and are extensively used in software like Adobe Illustrator. Unlike raster (bitmap) graphics, which are composed of individual pixels, vector graphics are based on mathematical equations that define shapes, lines, curves, and colors. This unique characteristic makes vector graphics highly versatile and resolution-independent, as they can be scaled up or down without losing image quality.

Key Concepts in Vector Graphics:

Points, Lines, and Paths: Vector graphics are built from fundamental elements like points, lines, and paths. Points are the building blocks that define positions in space. Lines are formed by connecting points, and paths are combinations of lines and curves that create complex shapes.

Curves and Bezier Curves: Curves are essential in creating smooth, organic shapes. Bezier curves are a type of curve that's widely used in vector graphics. They are defined by control points that determine the direction and curvature of the curve.

Anchors and Control Points: Anchors are points that define the endpoints of a path segment. Control points are used to manipulate the shape and direction of a curve between two anchors, allowing for precise control over curves.

Fill and Stroke: In vector graphics, shapes have both fill and stroke properties. The fill is the interior color or pattern of a shape, while the stroke is the outline. These properties can be customized with various colors, gradients, patterns, and line styles.

Paths and Compound Paths: Paths are sequences of connected lines and curves that define a shape. Compound paths are paths that share a boundary and can be treated as a single object. This is particularly useful when creating complex shapes with overlapping components.

Adobe Illustrator and Vector Graphics:

Adobe Illustrator is a powerful vector graphics software widely used by designers, illustrators, and artists. It provides a comprehensive set of tools and features that allow users to create intricate and visually appealing vector artwork.

Chapter 5 of the book delves into the exploration of Adobe Illustrator's capabilities, offering an overview of the following key aspects:

Workspace and Tools: Adobe Illustrator provides a versatile workspace equipped with various tools for creating and editing vector graphics. The chapter likely covers the selection tools, pen tool, shape tools, and transformation tools.

Drawing and Editing: Illustrator's drawing tools enable users to create shapes and paths. The Pen tool, in particular, plays a crucial role in drawing precise paths and curves. The chapter might explain how to create basic shapes and manipulate their properties.

Layers and Groups: Organizing artwork is essential for complex designs. Illustrator allows users to organize objects into layers and groups, making it easier to manage different elements of a design.

Color and Swatches: The chapter may discuss the use of color in vector graphics, including the Color panel, swatches, gradients, and patterns. Adobe Illustrator provides various ways to apply and manipulate color for creating visually appealing artwork.

Typography: Illustrator isn't just about shapes; it's also a robust tool for working with text. Users can create and customize text elements using a wide range of typography tools.

Effects and Filters: Adobe Illustrator offers a plethora of effects and filters that can be applied to vector objects to enhance their appearance. These can include blurs, shadows, glows, and distortions.

Exporting and Formats: The chapter might touch on how to save and export vector graphics in various formats, including SVG (Scalable Vector Graphics), PDF (Portable Document Format), and AI (Adobe Illustrator's native format).

Conclusion:

Understanding the fundamentals of vector graphics is crucial for working effectively with software like Adobe Illustrator. These graphics are composed of points, lines, and paths, allowing for scalable and resolution-independent designs. Adobe Illustrator empowers users to create intricate vector artwork using its diverse set of tools and features, which are likely discussed in Chapter 5 of the book. By mastering these fundamentals, designers can produce visually appealing and versatile artwork for a variety of applications.

QUIZ

Question 1:

Which of the following is a fundamental characteristic of vector graphics?

A) Composed of pixels

B) Resolution-dependent

C) Based on mathematical equations

D) Only suitable for photographs

Answer: C) Based on mathematical equations

Question 2:

In vector graphics, what are control points used for?

A) Determining the color of a shape

B) Defining the endpoints of a path

C) Manipulating the shape and direction of a curve

D) Creating pixel-based images

Answer: C) Manipulating the shape and direction of a curve

Question 3:

What is the purpose of a compound path in Adobe Illustrator?

A) To combine multiple layers

B) To group objects for easy selection

C) To create complex shapes with overlapping components

D) To apply special effects to paths

Answer: C) To create complex shapes with overlapping components

Question 4:

Which tool is commonly used in Adobe Illustrator to draw precise paths and curves?

A) Brush tool

B) Pencil tool

C) Shape tool

D) Pen tool

Answer: D) Pen tool

Question 5:

What are the two main properties of a vector shape in Adobe Illustrator?

A) Background and border

B) Fill and stroke

C) Brightness and contrast

D) Texture and opacity

Answer: B) Fill and stroke

Question 6:

What does the term "resolution-independent" mean in the context of vector graphics?

A) Images can be only viewed on high-resolution displays

B) Images can be scaled up without losing quality

C) Images can only be printed at a specific resolution

D) Images can only be created in certain sizes

Answer: B) Images can be scaled up without losing quality

Question 7:

Which Adobe Illustrator feature is used for organizing elements into separate visual layers?

A) Grouping

B) Clipping Mask

C) Compound Path

D) Layers Panel

Answer: D) Layers Panel

Question 8:

What format is commonly used to save vector graphics that can be easily displayed on websites?

A) JPG

B) GIF

C) PNG

D) SVG

Answer: D) SVG

Creating logos and illustrations

Introduction to Creating Logos and Illustrations:

Creating logos and illustrations is one of the most essential and common applications of Adobe Illustrator. Logos serve as the visual identity of a brand, while illustrations enhance visual storytelling in various media. In Chapter 5, you will delve into the techniques and tools Adobe Illustrator offers for crafting captivating logos and illustrations.

Key Concepts for Creating Logos and Illustrations:

Conceptualization: Before starting any design, it's crucial to have a clear understanding of the brand or message you're trying to convey. This involves brainstorming ideas, researching the target audience, and defining the core values or narrative.

Simplicity: Logos and illustrations often need to be recognizable at various sizes and across different platforms. Keeping the designs simple and minimizing intricate details ensures versatility and effective communication.

Shapes and Geometry: Basic shapes are the building blocks of many logos and illustrations. Adobe Illustrator's shape tools enable you to create circles, squares, triangles, and more, which can be combined and manipulated to form complex designs.

Custom Paths and Curves: The Pen tool is essential for creating custom paths and curves. Logos and illustrations frequently involve unique shapes that can be meticulously drawn using control points and anchor points.

Typography: Incorporating text is common in logos and some illustrations. Adobe Illustrator offers a wide range of typography tools to manipulate fonts, spacing, alignment, and more.

Color and Composition: Choosing the right color palette is crucial for conveying the desired emotions and associations. Proper composition ensures that elements are balanced and the design is visually appealing.

Creating Logos:

Simplicity and Memorability: Effective logos are simple and easily memorable. Think of iconic logos like Apple's apple or Nike's swoosh. They're simple shapes that represent the brand's essence.

Scalability: Logos appear on various mediums, from business cards to billboards. Vector-based logos created in Adobe Illustrator can be scaled up or down without losing quality.

Color Choice: Colors evoke emotions and associations. The color scheme should align with the brand's identity and values.

Versatility: Logos need to work in different color modes (color, grayscale, black and white) and backgrounds. Illustrator's transparency and layer modes aid in achieving this versatility.

Creating Illustrations:

Visual Storytelling: Illustrations help convey narratives visually. Whether in books, websites, or presentations, illustrations enhance storytelling and engage the audience.

Character Design: Creating characters requires attention to proportion, anatomy, and expressiveness. Adobe Illustrator's tools enable you to manipulate paths and shapes to achieve the desired character design.

Texturing and Detail: Illustrator offers techniques for adding texture and detail to illustrations, whether through gradients, patterns, or shading.

Dynamic Compositions: Illustrations often involve dynamic compositions that guide the viewer's eye and create visual interest. Understanding composition principles like rule of thirds and leading lines is valuable.

Adobe Illustrator Tools for Logos and Illustrations:

Shape Tools: Illustrator's shape tools help create basic forms that can be combined into more complex designs.

Pen Tool: The Pen tool is essential for drawing custom paths and curves, enabling precise control over shapes.

Type Tools: Illustrator's typography tools enable the incorporation of text into logos and illustrations.

Color Panel and Swatches: These tools facilitate color selection and management, ensuring a consistent color palette.

Pathfinder and Shapebuilder: These tools allow you to combine, subtract, and manipulate shapes, which is valuable for creating unique designs.

Conclusion:

Chapter 5 of "Exploring Adobe Illustrator" covers the intricacies of creating logos and illustrations using the powerful tools and features provided by Adobe Illustrator. By understanding design principles, conceptualization, and Illustrator's tools, you can craft impactful logos that represent brands and engaging illustrations that enhance visual storytelling across various media.

QUIZ

Question 1:

What is the primary purpose of a logo?

A) To tell a story

B) To showcase detailed artwork

C) To visually represent a brand or identity

D) To create abstract designs

Answer: C) To visually represent a brand or identity

Question 2:

Why is simplicity important when designing logos?

A) It saves time in the design process.

B) It allows for intricate details to be added.

C) Simple logos are easier to remember and recognize.

D) Complexity is outdated in modern design.

Answer: C) Simple logos are easier to remember and recognize.

Question 3:

What tool in Adobe Illustrator is essential for creating custom paths and curves?

A) Brush tool

B) Pencil tool

C) Shape tool

D) Pen tool

Answer: D) Pen tool

Question 4:

Why is scalability crucial for logos?

A) To accommodate different fonts and typography.

B) To ensure the logo can be printed in high resolution.

C) To allow the logo to be resized without losing quality.

D) To create different versions of the logo.

Answer: C) To allow the logo to be resized without losing quality.

Question 5:

Which aspect of color is important when creating a logo?

A) Using as many colors as possible.

B) Using trendy colors regardless of brand identity.

C) Selecting colors that align with the brand's identity and values.

D) Choosing colors randomly.

Answer: C) Selecting colors that align with the brand's identity and values.

Question 6:

What is the role of typography in logo design?

A) To showcase intricate lettering styles.

B) To add complexity to the logo.

C) To communicate a brand's message and identity.

D) To make the logo more colorful.

Answer: C) To communicate a brand's message and identity.

Question 7:

What is the benefit of using Adobe Illustrator's shape tools when creating illustrations?

A) They automatically generate complex shapes.

B) They provide realistic textures for objects.

C) They simplify the illustration process by limiting options.

D) They help create basic forms that can be combined into more complex designs.

Answer: D) They help create basic forms that can be combined into more complex designs.

Question 8:

What does the term "visual storytelling" refer to in the context of illustrations?

A) Using only visuals without any text.

B) Creating designs without any clear message.

C) Conveying narratives through visual elements.

D) Focusing solely on aesthetics without considering content.

Answer: C) Conveying narratives through visual elements.

Chapter 6: Mastering Adobe InDesign

Layout design for print and digital media

In the realm of graphic design, layout design is a crucial aspect that bridges the gap between creativity and functionality. It involves arranging visual elements, such as text, images, and graphics, in a harmonious and visually appealing manner to convey information effectively and engage the audience. Adobe InDesign, a powerful desktop publishing software, has become a staple tool for both print and digital layout design. Chapter 6 of your guidebook, "Mastering Adobe InDesign," delves into the intricacies of creating layouts for both print and digital media using this versatile tool.

I. Understanding the Basics:

The chapter begins by introducing the fundamental concepts of layout design. These concepts apply to both print and digital media, although there are specific considerations for each medium. Readers are guided through the principles of alignment, proximity, contrast, repetition, and balance. These principles play a pivotal role in creating visually appealing and easy-to-follow layouts.

II. Print Layout Design:

The chapter then delves into print layout design. Designing for print requires meticulous attention to detail due to the fixed dimensions of the physical medium. The chapter covers essential topics:

Page Setup and Margins: Readers learn how to set up page dimensions, margins, and bleeds. Bleeds are crucial for ensuring that images extend beyond the page edge, safeguarding against any slight misalignment during printing.

Typography: Typography is a cornerstone of print design. The chapter covers font selection, line spacing, kerning, and tracking. It explains how to maintain readability while achieving a visually pleasing balance of text elements.

Image Placement: The chapter provides insights into placing high-resolution images, graphics, and illustrations within the layout. It explains the importance of resolution, color modes, and image formats for optimal print quality.

Color Management: Understanding color spaces, such as CMYK for print, is essential to ensure accurate color reproduction. The chapter teaches readers how to manage color profiles and maintain color consistency across different devices and outputs.

Master Pages: Readers are introduced to the concept of master pages, which offer a way to maintain consistent design elements (like headers, footers, and page numbers) across multiple pages. This streamlines the design process and ensures a cohesive look throughout the document.

III. Digital Layout Design:

The chapter then transitions to digital layout design, focusing on the unique requirements of digital platforms such as websites, e-books, and interactive PDFs:

Responsive Design: Designing for various screen sizes and orientations is essential in the digital realm. The chapter guides readers through responsive design principles, enabling them to create layouts that adapt seamlessly to different devices.

Interactive Elements: Interactivity is a hallmark of digital design. Readers learn how to incorporate hyperlinks, buttons, animations, and multimedia elements into their layouts to enhance user engagement.

Web-safe Fonts and CSS: Font selection for digital layouts must consider web-safe fonts and the integration of CSS

(Cascading Style Sheets). The chapter explains how to embed fonts and use CSS to control typography and layout on web platforms.

Export Options: Different digital platforms require specific export settings. The chapter covers how to export designs as interactive PDFs, web-ready images, or e-book formats while maintaining design integrity.

IV. Bridging the Gap: Hybrid Designs:

Lastly, the chapter explores the convergence of print and digital design in hybrid formats, such as interactive PDFs with print-like layouts. This section encourages readers to think creatively and adapt their skills to evolving design trends.

In conclusion, Chapter 6 of "Mastering Adobe InDesign" provides a comprehensive guide to layout design for both print and digital media. By covering essential principles, tools, and techniques, the chapter equips readers with the skills to create compelling and effective layouts that captivate audiences, whether in the physical or digital realm.

QUIZ

Question 1:

Which design principle involves arranging visual elements in a way that establishes a connection between them and guides the viewer's eye through the layout?

a) Alignment

b) Proximity

c) Repetition

d) Balance

Answer: d) Balance

Question 2:

For print layouts, what is the purpose of including bleeds in your design?

a) To add visual interest

b) To adjust image resolution

c) To extend images beyond the page edge

d) To create interactive elements

Answer: c) To extend images beyond the page edge

Question 3:

What is the primary consideration when selecting fonts for digital layout design?

a) Typeface popularity

b) Personal preference

c) Web-safe fonts

d) Print-quality fonts

Answer: c) Web-safe fonts

Question 4:

Which design element is crucial for creating consistent headers, footers, and page numbers across multiple pages in both print and digital layouts?

a) Typography

b) Color profiles

c) Responsive design

d) Master pages

Answer: d) Master pages

Question 5:

What color mode is typically used for print layout design to ensure accurate color reproduction?

a) RGB

b) CMYK

c) HEX

d) Pantone

Answer: b) CMYK

Question 6:

What is the term for designing layouts that adapt seamlessly to different screen sizes and orientations in the digital realm?

a) Interactive design

b) Adaptive design

c) Responsive design

d) Hybrid design

Answer: c) Responsive design

Question 7:

What is the purpose of incorporating interactive elements like hyperlinks and animations in digital layouts?

a) To increase the file size

b) To improve typography

c) To enhance user engagement

d) To adjust color profiles

Answer: c) To enhance user engagement

Creating brochures, magazines, and eBooks

In the digital age, the design landscape has expanded to include a variety of formats, each requiring its own unique approach. Chapter 6 of "Mastering Adobe InDesign" dives into the intricate process of creating brochures, magazines, and eBooks using Adobe InDesign. These three formats serve different purposes and cater to diverse audiences, and this chapter equips designers with the knowledge and skills needed to craft captivating and effective content in each medium.

I. Brochures:

A brochure is a printed piece of marketing collateral that aims to convey information about a product, service, or event. The chapter begins by discussing the essentials of brochure design:

Layout Structure: The chapter guides designers through selecting appropriate brochure dimensions and folding styles, such as bi-fold, tri-fold, or gate-fold. It emphasizes the importance of planning the layout to accommodate content and imagery effectively.

Content Hierarchy: Designers learn to establish a clear content hierarchy, placing essential information prominently while ensuring a visually pleasing flow. This involves using headlines, subheadings, bullet points, and call-to-action elements strategically.

Imagery and Graphics: The chapter explains how to choose high-quality images that resonate with the brochure's message. It delves into image cropping, resizing, and image placement techniques to maintain visual appeal.

Color and Typography: Designers are introduced to the significance of color psychology and typography choices in conveying the intended message. The chapter advises on selecting fonts that align with the brand's identity and maintaining consistency in color schemes.

II. Magazines:

Magazine design requires a balance between captivating visuals and organized content. The chapter transitions to magazine design, addressing the following key points:

Grid Systems: The chapter delves into grid systems, which are essential for organizing complex magazine layouts. Designers learn to establish consistent column structures that facilitate content placement and maintain readability.

Article Layout: Readers are guided through designing compelling article layouts that incorporate text, images, pull quotes, and captions. The chapter emphasizes the importance of establishing visual hierarchy and white space to enhance the reading experience.

Continuity and Flow: Creating a seamless flow throughout the magazine is vital. The chapter introduces techniques such as page numbering, consistent styling, and thematic consistency to ensure a cohesive reading journey.

Cover Design: Designers explore cover design strategies that aim to capture attention and reflect the magazine's essence. This includes creating eye-catching headlines, dynamic imagery, and strong branding elements.

III. eBooks:

eBooks offer a digital platform for sharing long-form content, whether it's fiction, non-fiction, or educational material. The chapter concludes by addressing the intricacies of eBook design:

Responsive Design: As eBooks are viewed on various devices, responsive design is crucial. Designers learn to create layouts that adapt to different screen sizes and orientations, ensuring a consistent reading experience.

Interactive Elements: eBooks allow for interactive elements such as hyperlinks, multimedia, and animations. The chapter provides guidance on incorporating these elements to enhance user engagement and understanding.

eBook Formats: Different eBook formats exist, each with specific requirements. The chapter discusses the importance of exporting to formats such as EPUB and PDF, while maintaining design integrity and functionality.

Font Embedding: Designers discover how to embed fonts in eBooks, enabling consistent typography across various devices. This ensures that the chosen fonts are displayed as intended, even if they're not native to the reading device.

In conclusion, Chapter 6 of "Mastering Adobe InDesign" equips designers with the skills necessary to create brochures, magazines, and eBooks that effectively communicate information, engage audiences, and maintain design integrity across various formats. By understanding the nuances of each medium and harnessing the capabilities of Adobe InDesign, designers can confidently embark on creating content that resonates in the print and digital realms.

QUIZ

Question 1:

What is the primary purpose of a brochure?

a) To share fictional stories

b) To provide in-depth research

c) To convey information about products or services

d) To showcase artistic illustrations

Answer: c) To convey information about products or services

Question 2:

Which folding style involves dividing a brochure into three panels, often used for presenting content in a compact format?

a) Bi-fold

b) Tri-fold

c) Gate-fold

d) Z-fold

Answer: b) Tri-fold

Question 3:

In magazine design, what is the purpose of establishing a grid system?

a) To organize complex layouts

b) To add decorative elements

c) To insert interactive multimedia

d) To embed fonts for consistent typography

Answer: a) To organize complex layouts

Question 4:

What does responsive design refer to in eBook creation?

a) Adding interactive animations

b) Incorporating multimedia elements

c) Designing for various screen sizes and orientations

d) Embedding fonts for consistent typography

Answer: c) Designing for various screen sizes and orientations

Question 5:

What interactive elements can be included in eBooks to enhance user engagement?

a) Page numbers

b) Table of contents

c) Typography styles

d) Hyperlinks and multimedia

Answer: d) Hyperlinks and multimedia

Question 6:

What is the purpose of maintaining continuity and flow in magazine design?

a) To create visually complex layouts

b) To enhance the cover design

c) To engage readers with multimedia

d) To ensure a cohesive reading experience

Answer: d) To ensure a cohesive reading experience

Question 7:

Which design element is crucial for creating an eye-catching magazine cover?

a) Consistent styling

b) Grid system

c) Page numbering

d) Embedding fonts

Answer: a) Consistent styling

Chapter 7: Video Editing with Adobe Premiere Pro

Basics of video editing and timeline usage

In the world of modern digital content creation, video editing plays a crucial role in shaping raw footage into polished and engaging visual narratives. Adobe Premiere Pro, one of the industry-standard video editing software, empowers editors to bring their creative visions to life. Chapter 7 of your guide delves into the basics of video editing using Adobe Premiere Pro, focusing on fundamental concepts and the effective utilization of the timeline.

1. Introduction to Video Editing:

Video editing is the process of manipulating and rearranging video clips to create a coherent and compelling story. This involves removing unwanted segments, arranging clips in a meaningful sequence, adding transitions, effects, titles, and more. Adobe Premiere Pro is renowned for its versatile set of tools that facilitate these tasks.

2. The Timeline:

The timeline is the heart of your video editing workspace. It's where you arrange and organize your video and audio clips to create a seamless flow. Adobe Premiere Pro's timeline provides multiple tracks for video, audio, effects, and more, allowing you to layer different elements of your project.

3. Importing Footage:

Before you can start editing, you need to import your video and audio files into Adobe Premiere Pro. This is done through the Media Browser or by simply dragging and dropping files into the project panel.

4. Creating a New Project:

When you start a new project, you define settings such as resolution, frame rate, and aspect ratio. These settings should match the specifications of your footage to ensure the best quality.

5. Basics of Timeline Usage:

Arranging Clips: Drag and drop your video and audio clips onto the timeline. Use the Selection Tool (V) to move and manipulate clips on the timeline.

Trimming Clips: Use the Razor Tool (C) to cut clips at specific points. The Selection Tool allows you to select and delete unwanted sections.

Timeline Zooming: Zoom in and out on the timeline using the zoom slider or keyboard shortcuts to work more precisely.

Snapping: Turn on snapping to make sure clips align accurately on the timeline, creating seamless transitions.

6. Editing Techniques:

Cutting and Splicing: Cut unwanted sections and splice together desired clips to create a cohesive flow.

Transitions: Add transitions (dissolves, cuts, wipes, etc.) between clips to smoothen jumps between scenes.

Audio Mixing: Adjust audio levels to ensure consistent sound throughout your video.

Effects and Color Correction: Enhance your video by applying effects and adjusting color and brightness.

7. Working with Audio:

Audio Tracks: Use audio tracks on the timeline to layer different audio elements such as dialogue, music, and sound effects.

Audio Effects: Apply audio effects like EQ, compression, and noise reduction to improve audio quality.

8. Adding Titles and Graphics:

Adobe Premiere Pro allows you to create and add titles, lower thirds, and graphics to enhance your video's visual appeal. You can create these elements within the software or import them from other sources.

9. Exporting Your Project:

Once your editing is complete, you need to export your project into a final video file. Adobe Premiere Pro offers various export presets, but you can also customize settings like resolution, format, and bitrate according to your needs.

10. Saving Your Project:

It's crucial to save your project regularly to prevent any loss of work. Adobe Premiere Pro creates project files that store your editing decisions, so you can always return to your project and make changes.

Chapter 7 provides a foundational understanding of video editing using Adobe Premiere Pro. From assembling clips on the timeline to adding effects and exporting your final product, this chapter equips you with the knowledge to start creating engaging videos with confidence. Remember, video editing is a skill that improves with practice, so don't hesitate to experiment and explore the software's features to unleash your creativity.

QUIZ

Question 1: What is the primary purpose of video editing in Adobe Premiere Pro?

A) Adding special effects

B) Organizing project files

C) Manipulating raw footage into a coherent narrative

D) Enhancing audio quality

Answer: C) Manipulating raw footage into a coherent narrative

Question 2: Which Adobe Premiere Pro tool is used to cut clips at specific points on the timeline?

A) Selection Tool (V)

B) Razor Tool (C)

C) Pen Tool (P)

D) Move Tool (M)

Answer: B) Razor Tool (C)

Question 3: What does the timeline in Adobe Premiere Pro allow you to do?

A) Browse media files

B) Import audio files only

C) Arrange and organize video, audio, and effects on tracks

D) Apply video effects only

Answer: C) Arrange and organize video, audio, and effects on tracks

Question 4: Which function of Adobe Premiere Pro ensures that clips align accurately on the timeline?

A) Snapping

B) Trimming

C) Panning

D) Masking

Answer: A) Snapping

Question 5: What should you define when starting a new project in Adobe Premiere Pro?

A) The final export resolution only

B) The frame rate and audio settings only

C) Settings that match the specifications of your footage

D) The file format for exporting

Answer: C) Settings that match the specifications of your footage

Question 6: Which tool in Adobe Premiere Pro is used to adjust audio levels and ensure consistent sound throughout the video?

A) Selection Tool (V)

B) Pen Tool (P)

C) Audio Mixer Tool (A)

D) Razor Tool (C)

Answer: C) Audio Mixer Tool (A)

Question 7: What is the final step after completing video editing in Adobe Premiere Pro?

A) Arranging clips on the timeline

B) Adding transitions and effects

C) Exporting the project into a video file

D) Importing audio files

Answer: C) Exporting the project into a video file

Adding effects, transitions, and titles

In the realm of video editing, enhancing the visual appeal of your content is crucial to capturing your audience's attention and conveying your narrative effectively. Adobe Premiere Pro provides an array of tools and features that allow you to add effects, transitions, and titles to your videos, enriching their overall quality and storytelling impact. Chapter 7 of your guide explores the process of incorporating these elements into your projects.

1. Adding Effects:

Effects in Adobe Premiere Pro refer to adjustments applied to clips that modify their visual and auditory characteristics. These can range from basic color correction to more advanced visual enhancements. Here's how you can add effects to your clips:

Applying Effects: Select a clip on the timeline, then navigate to the "Effects" panel. Choose an effect category (e.g., "Color Correction," "Video Effects") and drag the desired effect onto the clip.

Adjusting Effect Parameters: Once an effect is applied, you can modify its settings in the "Effect Controls" panel. This allows you to fine-tune the effect's intensity, duration, and other attributes.

2. Using Transitions:

Transitions are essential for creating smooth and engaging transitions between clips. They help eliminate abrupt cuts and create a more visually pleasing flow between scenes. Adobe Premiere Pro offers various transition options:

Adding Transitions: To apply a transition, drag and drop it between two adjacent clips on the timeline. Transitions can be found in the "Effects" panel under the "Video Transitions" category.

Customizing Transitions: After adding a transition, you can adjust its duration and other properties in the "Effect Controls" panel. This allows you to control the timing and behavior of the transition.

3. Incorporating Titles and Graphics:

Titles and graphics play a vital role in providing context, information, and branding within your videos. Adobe Premiere Pro enables you to create and customize these elements directly within the software:

Adding Titles: To add a title, navigate to the "Graphics" workspace and choose the "Essential Graphics" panel. Here, you can select from a range of pre-designed title templates or create custom titles with text, shapes, and images.

Customizing Titles: After adding a title, use the "Essential Graphics" panel to modify text, font, size, color, and animation effects. This ensures that titles seamlessly integrate into your video's aesthetic.

4. Keyframing:

Keyframing is the process of setting specific values for an effect or property at specific points in time. This technique is useful for creating dynamic animations and gradual changes. In Adobe Premiere Pro, you can apply keyframes to effects, transformations, and other parameters:

Adding Keyframes: Select a clip or effect property on the timeline, navigate to the "Effect Controls" panel, and click the stopwatch icon next to the parameter you want to animate. This adds a keyframe at the current playhead position.

Adjusting Keyframes: Move the playhead to different points in the timeline and adjust the effect's parameters to create smooth transitions between keyframes.

Chapter 7's focus on adding effects, transitions, and titles in Adobe Premiere Pro empowers you to elevate your video content to new creative heights. By experimenting with different effects, transitions, and title designs, you can tailor your videos to match your unique style and effectively communicate your message to your audience. Remember that these elements are tools for enhancing your storytelling, so use them thoughtfully to convey your narrative effectively.

QUIZ

Question 1: What is the purpose of adding transitions between video clips in Adobe Premiere Pro?

A) To apply color correction to clips

B) To create smooth transitions between scenes

C) To adjust audio levels

D) To crop and resize clips

Answer: B) To create smooth transitions between scenes

Question 2: Where can you find transitions in Adobe Premiere Pro for adding to your video clips?

A) "Effect Controls" panel

B) "Graphics" workspace

C) "Video Transitions" category in the "Effects" panel

D) "Essential Graphics" panel

Answer: C) "Video Transitions" category in the "Effects" panel

Question 3: What is keyframing used for in Adobe Premiere Pro?

A) Adding titles and graphics

B) Applying color correction

C) Adjusting audio levels

D) Creating dynamic animations and gradual changes

Answer: D) Creating dynamic animations and gradual changes

Question 4: How can you customize the appearance of titles in Adobe Premiere Pro?

A) By using the Razor Tool

B) By adjusting audio levels

C) By adding keyframes

D) By using the "Essential Graphics" panel

Answer: D) By using the "Essential Graphics" panel

Question 5: What is the purpose of applying effects to video clips in Adobe Premiere Pro?

A) To add transitions between clips

B) To rearrange the order of clips on the timeline

C) To adjust the audio levels of clips

D) To modify the visual and auditory characteristics of clips

Answer: D) To modify the visual and auditory characteristics of clips

Question 6: How can you adjust the duration of a transition between two clips in Adobe Premiere Pro?

A) By dragging and dropping the transition onto the timeline

B) By using the "Essential Graphics" panel

C) By applying keyframes to the transition

D) By adjusting the transition's properties in the "Effect Controls" panel

Answer: D) By adjusting the transition's properties in the "Effect Controls" panel

Question 7: Which panel in Adobe Premiere Pro allows you to add and customize titles, text, shapes, and images?

A) "Effect Controls" panel

B) "Graphics" workspace

C) "Video Transitions" category in the "Effects" panel

D) "Essential Graphics" panel

Answer: D) "Essential Graphics" panel

Chapter 8: Adobe After Effects for Motion Graphics

Introduction to motion graphics and animation

Motion graphics and animation have become integral parts of visual communication, spanning from film and television to web content and advertisements. They allow designers and creators to bring ideas to life, convey complex information, and captivate audiences through dynamic visuals. In this chapter, we delve into the fundamentals of motion graphics and animation, focusing on how they are applied using the powerful software tool: Adobe After Effects.

I. Understanding Motion Graphics and Animation:

Motion Graphics: Motion graphics refer to the art of combining graphic design, typography, and visual effects to create compelling, dynamic visuals that convey information, tell stories, and evoke emotions. Unlike traditional static graphics, motion graphics involve movement, transitions, and transformations, making them more engaging and attention-grabbing.

Animation: Animation, on the other hand, is the technique of creating the illusion of movement through the rapid display of a sequence of static images. It encompasses a wide range of styles and techniques, from traditional hand-drawn animation to modern computer-generated animation. Motion graphics often utilize animation principles to achieve fluid and realistic movements.

II. Adobe After Effects:

Adobe After Effects: Adobe After Effects is a professional-grade software used extensively in the motion graphics and visual effects industries. It enables designers to create intricate animations, stunning visual effects, and captivating motion graphics by combining various elements such as text, images, videos, and effects.

III. Key Concepts in Motion Graphics and Animation:

1. Timeline and Keyframes: The timeline in After Effects is where animations are crafted. Keyframes are markers that define specific points in time where properties of elements, such as position, opacity, and scale, are set. Animators set keyframes to create changes over time, giving the illusion of movement.

2. Easing: Easing refers to the acceleration or deceleration of an animation's movement to make it more natural and appealing. It prevents abrupt and robotic-looking transitions by adding a sense of inertia and flow.

3. Motion Paths: Motion paths are the trajectories along which elements move. By manipulating motion paths, designers can create intricate movements and transitions, allowing objects to follow specific trajectories.

4. Effects and Presets: After Effects offers a vast array of effects and presets that can be applied to elements to achieve various visual styles and transformations. These effects can range from simple color corrections to complex particle simulations.

5. Parenting and Hierarchies: Elements can be parented to other elements, creating a hierarchy. When the parent moves or transforms, its child elements follow suit. This is particularly useful for creating complex animations involving multiple objects.

6. Text and Typography: After Effects allows for advanced text animations, enabling designers to animate individual characters or entire blocks of text. This feature is invaluable

for creating engaging title sequences, lower thirds, and kinetic typography.

IV. Applying Motion Graphics and Animation:

1. Title Sequences: Motion graphics are frequently used in the opening credits of films and TV shows, where animated text and visuals set the tone for the story.

2. Infographics and Data Visualization: Complex data and information can be transformed into visually appealing and easily digestible animations, enhancing understanding and engagement.

3. Advertisements and Promotions: Motion graphics are commonly used in commercials to showcase products, services, or concepts in an engaging and memorable manner.

4. User Interfaces (UI) and User Experience (UX) Design: Motion graphics enhance the usability and aesthetics of digital interfaces, guiding users through interactions and transitions.

5. Visual Effects: After Effects is extensively used in the creation of visual effects for films, TV shows, and commercials. It allows for the integration of live-action

footage with computer-generated elements, creating seamless and captivating visuals.

V. Conclusion:

Motion graphics and animation are powerful tools that enable designers and creators to convey ideas and messages in ways that capture attention and resonate with audiences. Adobe After Effects serves as a versatile platform for bringing these concepts to life, allowing designers to explore their creativity and craft stunning animations and motion graphics that leave a lasting impact. As technology advances and creative possibilities expand, motion graphics and animation continue to evolve, shaping the way we perceive and interact with visual content.

QUIZ

Question 1: What are motion graphics?

A) Still images used in animation.

B) The art of combining graphic design and visual effects to create dynamic visuals.

C) Videos without any movement or transitions.

D) Traditional hand-drawn animations.

Answer: B) The art of combining graphic design and visual effects to create dynamic visuals.

Question 2: What is the purpose of easing in animation?

A) Adding more keyframes to the animation.

B) Increasing the speed of animation.

C) Creating abrupt transitions for a dynamic effect.

D) Making animation movement more natural and smooth.

Answer: D) Making animation movement more natural and smooth.

Question 3: Which software is extensively used for creating motion graphics and animations?

A) Microsoft Word

B) Adobe After Effects

C) Google Chrome

D) Microsoft Excel

Answer: B) Adobe After Effects

Question 4: What are keyframes used for in animation?

A) Enhancing color and lighting.

B) Creating transitions between scenes.

C) Defining specific points in time with certain element properties.

D) Adding sound effects to animations.

Answer: C) Defining specific points in time with certain element properties.

Question 5: Motion paths in animation refer to:

A) The paths that characters walk along in a storyline.

B) The paths that the camera follows during a scene.

C) Trajectories along which elements move.

D) The flow of the narrative in an animated movie.

Answer: C) Trajectories along which elements move.

Question 6: What is the benefit of parenting in animation?

A) It adds special effects to animations.

B) It creates more keyframes for complex animations.

C) It allows elements to move independently.

D) It creates a hierarchy where child elements follow the movement of parent elements.

Answer: D) It creates a hierarchy where child elements follow the movement of parent elements.

Question 7: In motion graphics, what does the term "kinetic typography" refer to?

A) Typography that remains static throughout the animation.

B) Typography with varying font sizes and styles.

C) Typography that moves and animates in sync with the audio or other elements.

D) Typography with three-dimensional effects.

Answer: C) Typography that moves and animates in sync with the audio or other elements.

Creating visual effects and cinematic animations

Visual effects (VFX) and cinematic animations are essential elements in modern filmmaking, advertising, and digital content creation. Adobe After Effects, a powerful software tool, plays a central role in bringing these effects to life. In this chapter, we explore how After Effects is used to create captivating visual effects and cinematic animations.

I. Visual Effects (VFX) and Cinematic Animations:

Visual Effects (VFX): Visual effects involve the integration of live-action footage with computer-generated elements to create scenes and effects that are impractical or impossible to achieve during production. VFX can range from subtle enhancements like color correction to elaborate simulations of explosions, creatures, and fantastical environments.

Cinematic Animations: Cinematic animations refer to the art of creating dynamic and immersive animated sequences that contribute to the storytelling and emotional impact of a film.

These animations can include opening credits, action sequences, dream sequences, and more.

II. Adobe After Effects for VFX and Cinematic Animations:

1. Layer-based Compositing: After Effects uses a layer-based compositing approach, allowing artists to combine different visual elements such as images, videos, and effects on separate layers. This technique facilitates precise control over the composition and enables the creation of complex visual effects.

2. Effects and Presets: After Effects provides a wide range of effects and presets that can be applied to layers. These effects include particle systems, motion blur, distortion, and more. Presets are pre-configured effects settings that can be easily applied to elements for consistent visual styles.

3. Tracking and Stabilization: After Effects offers powerful tracking and stabilization tools. Tracking enables the software to follow the movement of objects in a scene, making it possible to attach elements to specific points in live-action footage. Stabilization helps eliminate camera shake in footage.

4. Green Screen (Chroma Key) Compositing: After Effects excels in green screen compositing, where actors are filmed in front of a green or blue screen and then composited onto different backgrounds or environments.

5. Particle Systems: Particle systems are used to simulate natural phenomena like fire, smoke, rain, and explosions. After Effects provides tools to control particle behavior, appearance, and movement.

III. Steps in Creating Visual Effects and Cinematic Animations:

1. Pre-production Planning: Determine the visual effects required for the project and plan how they will be integrated into the scenes. Consider factors like lighting, perspective, and camera movement.

2. Asset Creation: Create or gather the assets needed for the VFX, such as 3D models, images, videos, and audio elements.

3. Compositing: Use After Effects to composite the live-action footage and computer-generated elements. Apply effects, adjust colors, and ensure a seamless integration between the real and virtual elements.

4. Animation: Animate any elements that require movement, such as characters, objects, or visual effects like explosions.

5. Rendering: Render the composited scenes with all the visual effects and animations. This process can be time-consuming due to the complexity of the effects.

6. Post-production: In the final stages, fine-tune the effects, adjust timing, and make any necessary edits to achieve the desired cinematic look.

IV. Applications of VFX and Cinematic Animations:

1. Film and Television: Visual effects are widely used in movies and TV shows to create breathtaking environments, creatures, and action sequences.

2. Advertising and Promotions: Cinematic animations and VFX add impact to commercials and promotional videos, making them more memorable and engaging.

3. Music Videos: VFX and animations enhance the storytelling and visual appeal of music videos, creating immersive experiences.

4. Gaming: VFX and cinematic animations contribute to the realism and excitement of video games, enriching the player's experience.

V. Conclusion:

Visual effects and cinematic animations, powered by Adobe After Effects, bring imagination to life on the screen. The software's capabilities allow artists to seamlessly blend real-world footage with virtual elements, resulting in stunning and immersive visuals that captivate audiences across various mediums. As technology continues to advance, the possibilities for creating breathtaking VFX and cinematic animations only continue to expand, pushing the boundaries of creativity and storytelling in the world of visual media.

QUIZ

Question 1: What are visual effects (VFX) in filmmaking and animation?

A) Live-action sequences without any editing.

B) Computer-generated characters in a film.

C) The integration of live-action footage with computer-generated elements.

D) Audio effects used to enhance dialogues.

Answer: C) The integration of live-action footage with computer-generated elements.

Question 2: What is the primary purpose of layer-based compositing in Adobe After Effects?

A) Creating text-based animations.

B) Simulating realistic physics for animations.

C) Combining different visual elements on separate layers for complex compositions.

D) Applying color correction to videos.

Answer: C) Combining different visual elements on separate layers for complex compositions.

Question 3: Which tool in After Effects is used to follow the movement of objects in a scene and attach elements to specific points in live-action footage?

A) Particle system

B) Tracking

C) Stabilization

D) Keyframing

Answer: B) Tracking

Question 4: What is the purpose of using green screen (chroma key) compositing?

A) To create animations with a green color scheme.

B) To eliminate green color from images and videos.

C) To composite actors onto different backgrounds or environments.

D) To add motion blur to elements in a scene.

Answer: C) To composite actors onto different backgrounds or environments.

Question 5: What are particle systems commonly used for in visual effects?

A) Changing the aspect ratio of videos.

B) Adding cartoon-style animations to scenes.

C) Simulating natural phenomena like fire, smoke, and explosions.

D) Applying color grading to videos.

Answer: C) Simulating natural phenomena like fire, smoke, and explosions.

Question 6: In the context of creating visual effects, what does "rendering" refer to?

A) Adjusting the color balance of a video.

B) Adding special effects to a scene.

C) The process of creating a final video with all effects and animations.

D) Deleting unnecessary layers from a composition.

Answer: C) The process of creating a final video with all effects and animations.

Question 7: How do cinematic animations contribute to storytelling in films?

A) They create random visual effects.

B) They replace actors with computer-generated characters.

C) They add dynamic elements to the background of scenes.

D) They create dynamic and immersive animated sequences that enhance storytelling.

Answer: D) They create dynamic and immersive animated sequences that enhance storytelling.

Chapter 9: Web Design with Adobe XD

Prototyping and designing user interfaces

Prototyping is a crucial phase in the user interface (UI) design process. It involves creating interactive mockups of your design to test and validate the user experience before moving into the development phase. Adobe XD is a powerful tool that facilitates both designing and prototyping interfaces.

1. Understanding the Basics:

Wireframing: Begin by creating wireframes, which are basic, low-fidelity representations of the layout and structure of your web page. Wireframes help define the placement of elements without delving into visual details.

Design: Once your wireframes are in place, move on to designing the actual interface. This involves choosing colors, typography, images, and other visual elements that align with your brand and project goals.

2. Adobe XD Tools and Features:

Adobe XD offers a range of tools and features to aid in designing and prototyping web interfaces:

Artboards: These are like virtual canvases where you design individual screens or pages of your web application. You can create multiple artboards to represent different states of your interface.

Components: Components are reusable design elements that help maintain consistency throughout your design. For example, you can create a button component and use it across various screens.

Prototyping: Adobe XD enables you to create interactive prototypes by defining links, transitions, and interactions between different artboards. This allows you to simulate user flows and test how users will interact with your interface.

Animations: You can add animations to your prototype to simulate real-world interactions. This could include transitions like fades, slides, and overlays, which provide a more realistic view of how the final product will behave.

3. Designing for User Experience:

User-Centered Design: Always keep the end-users in mind. Consider their needs, preferences, and pain points as you design your interface. User research and personas can help inform your design decisions.

Navigation: Design an intuitive navigation system that allows users to easily move through your website. Use clear labels, organized menus, and consistent placement of navigation elements.

Visual Hierarchy: Arrange content in a way that guides users' attention. Use contrast, size, and spacing to emphasize important elements and create a hierarchy of information.

4. Prototyping for Testing:

Interactive Elements: Use Adobe XD's prototyping capabilities to create clickable elements. Test how buttons, links, and forms will function in the final product.

User Flows: Create prototypes that represent various user flows, such as signing up, making a purchase, or browsing a product catalog. This helps identify potential issues and refine the user experience.

User Testing: Share your interactive prototype with potential users or stakeholders to gather feedback. This can help you identify usability problems and make necessary improvements.

5. Iteration and Refinement:

Iterative Design: UI design is an iterative process. Gather feedback from user testing and stakeholders, and use it to refine your design. Make necessary adjustments based on the insights gained.

Consistency: Maintain visual consistency throughout your design. Elements like color schemes, typography, and spacing should remain consistent across different screens.

6. Exporting Assets:

Once your design is finalized and prototyping is complete, you can use Adobe XD's export features to generate assets that developers can use for actual web development. These assets may include images, icons, and design specifications.

7. Collaboration:

Adobe XD supports collaboration, allowing multiple designers and stakeholders to work on the same project simultaneously. This can streamline the design process and ensure everyone is on the same page.

8. Responsive Design:

Web design should consider various screen sizes and devices. Adobe XD allows you to create responsive designs by using features like responsive resize and breakpoints, ensuring that your interface looks and functions well on different devices.

QUIZ

Question: What is the primary purpose of prototyping in the UI design process?

a) Adding visual flair to the design

b) Testing and validating user interactions and experiences

c) Exporting design assets for development

d) Creating wireframes for marketing materials

Answer: b) Testing and validating user interactions and experiences

Question: In Adobe XD, what are components used for?

a) Creating high-fidelity designs

b) Adding animations to prototypes

c) Defining user flows

d) Reusable design elements for maintaining consistency

Answer: d) Reusable design elements for maintaining consistency

Question: What is an artboard in Adobe XD?

a) A tool for exporting design assets

b) An animation feature

c) A virtual canvas for designing individual screens or pages

d) A prototyping technique

Answer: c) A virtual canvas for designing individual screens or pages

Question: What is the purpose of creating interactive prototypes in Adobe XD?

a) To showcase design assets to stakeholders

b) To generate code for the final website

c) To simulate user interactions and test user flows

d) To create high-resolution images

Answer: c) To simulate user interactions and test user flows

Question: Which Adobe XD feature allows you to define links, transitions, and interactions between artboards?

a) Components

b) Artboards

c) Animations

d) Prototyping

Answer: d) Prototyping

Question: What does the term "user-centered design" refer to?

a) Designing solely based on the preferences of the designer

b) Designing according to the latest design trends

c) Designing with the primary focus on user needs and preferences

d) Designing without any consideration for usability

Answer: c) Designing with the primary focus on user needs and preferences

Question: Which Adobe XD feature supports collaboration among multiple designers and stakeholders working on the same project?

a) Exporting assets

b) Components

c) Responsive design

d) Collaborative editing

Answer: d) Collaborative editing

Question: What is the purpose of using responsive design principles in web design?

a) To create visually appealing designs

b) To ensure the website works only on certain devices

c) To adapt the design for different screen sizes and devices

d) To prioritize desktop users over mobile users

Answer: c) To adapt the design for different screen sizes and devices

Question: What phase of the design process involves refining the design based on feedback and insights gained from user testing?

a) Wireframing

b) User-centered design

c) Iterative design

d) Artboard creation

Answer: c) Iterative design

Question: How can interactive prototypes created with Adobe XD be useful for user testing?

a) They provide code snippets for developers

b) They offer high-resolution images for marketing materials

c) They allow testers to click through and experience user flows

d) They automatically generate responsive designs

Answer: c) They allow testers to click through and experience user flows

Creating interactive web and mobile app designs

Creating Interactive Web and Mobile App Designs

Interactive designs go beyond static visuals to provide users with a dynamic and engaging experience. This involves creating clickable prototypes that simulate user interactions and allow you to test and refine the user experience before development begins. Adobe XD offers a robust set of tools and features to aid in creating such interactive designs.

1. Understanding User Flows:

Before diving into the design process, it's essential to map out the user flows or journeys that users will take within your web or mobile app. This involves identifying key actions, transitions, and decision points that users will encounter. Understanding user flows helps in structuring your design and anticipating user needs.

2. Creating Artboards:

In Adobe XD, artboards serve as the canvas for your designs. Each artboard represents a screen or a state of your web or mobile app. You can create multiple artboards to illustrate different pages, screens, or stages of interaction.

3. Designing Interactive Elements:

Buttons: Design clickable buttons with appropriate labels and styling. These buttons represent actions that users can take, such as "Submit," "Next," or "Cancel."

Links: Create hyperlinks or navigational links to simulate transitions between screens or to external content.

Forms: Design interactive form fields like text inputs, checkboxes, and radio buttons. This helps simulate how users will input information.

Menus: Design drop-down menus, context menus, or navigation menus to demonstrate how users will navigate through your app.

4. Prototyping:

Adobe XD's prototyping mode enables you to create interactive prototypes by defining links and transitions between artboards. Here's how this process generally works:

Linking: Select an element (e.g., a button) on one artboard and define where it leads. This could be another artboard, an external website, or a specific interaction like an overlay.

Transitions: Specify the type of transition between artboards, such as slide, fade, or dissolve. These transitions mimic the actual movement from one screen to another.

Animations: Add animations to your interactions to make them more realistic. For instance, you can animate elements to slide in or fade out during transitions.

5. Microinteractions:

Microinteractions are subtle, yet important, interactions that enhance the user experience. They include things like button hover effects, loading animations, and error messages. Adobe XD allows you to prototype these microinteractions, providing a comprehensive view of the user experience.

6. Testing and Feedback:

Once you've created your interactive prototype, it's time to gather feedback and conduct user testing. Share the prototype with stakeholders, clients, or actual users to gather insights into the usability and effectiveness of your design.

7. Iterative Refinement:

Based on feedback and user testing results, iterate on your design to improve the user experience. Address any usability issues, navigation challenges, or design inconsistencies that arise during testing.

8. Sharing and Collaboration:

Adobe XD facilitates collaboration among design teams and stakeholders. Multiple users can work on the same project simultaneously, making it easier to brainstorm, make changes, and align on design decisions.

9. Responsive Design:

Consider different screen sizes and devices when creating interactive designs. Adobe XD offers responsive design features, allowing you to create designs that adapt well to various screen sizes and orientations.

10. Handoff to Developers:

Once the interactive design is finalized, Adobe XD offers features that streamline the handoff process to developers. You can generate design specs, assets, and code snippets that developers can use as a reference for building the actual app or website.

In conclusion, Chapter 9 of a guide on Web Design with Adobe XD would likely cover the process of creating interactive web and mobile app designs using Adobe XD's tools and features. It would emphasize the importance of user flows, designing interactive elements, prototyping, testing, iterative refinement, and collaboration. Remember to refer to the actual chapter for the most accurate and detailed information.

QUIZ

Question: What is the purpose of creating interactive prototypes in web and mobile app design?

a) To showcase design assets to stakeholders

b) To generate actual code for the final product

c) To simulate user interactions and test the user experience

d) To create high-resolution images for marketing

Answer: c) To simulate user interactions and test the user experience

Question: In Adobe XD, what are artboards used for?

a) Storing design assets like images and icons

b) Writing code for animations

c) Defining responsive design breakpoints

d) Representing different screens or states of an interface

Answer: d) Representing different screens or states of an interface

Question: Which Adobe XD feature allows you to define links and transitions between artboards for creating interactive prototypes?

a) Animations

b) Components

c) Artboard panels

d) Prototyping mode

Answer: d) Prototyping mode

Question: What are microinteractions in interactive design?

a) Subtle animations and effects that enhance user experience

b) Comprehensive user flows between screens

c) Large-scale animations that cover the entire interface

d) High-resolution images used for backgrounds

Answer: a) Subtle animations and effects that enhance user experience

Question: What is the purpose of conducting user testing on interactive prototypes?

a) To showcase design skills to potential clients

b) To generate ideas for new design projects

c) To gather feedback and insights on the usability of the design

d) To finalize the design without making any changes

Answer: c) To gather feedback and insights on the usability of the design

Question: How does responsive design contribute to the creation of interactive designs?

a) It focuses solely on aesthetics

b) It automates the prototyping process

c) It ensures that designs work well on various screen sizes and devices

d) It enhances the performance of interactive elements

Answer: c) It ensures that designs work well on various screen sizes and devices

Question: Which Adobe XD feature assists in sharing and collaboration among design teams and stakeholders?

a) Exporting assets

b) Handoff mode

c) Collaboration tools

d) Component libraries

Answer: c) Collaboration tools

Question: What is the primary benefit of creating clickable buttons, links, and forms in an interactive prototype?

a) They make the design visually appealing

b) They help in generating code for developers

c) They provide a dynamic experience for users to interact with

d) They minimize the need for user testing

Answer: c) They provide a dynamic experience for users to interact with

Question: What is the main purpose of defining transitions between artboards in a prototype?

a) To showcase different design concepts

b) To generate high-resolution images

c) To add visual flair to the design

d) To simulate the movement between different screens

Answer: d) To simulate the movement between different screens

Question: How does Adobe XD assist in the handoff process to developers after creating interactive designs?

a) It generates fully functional code

b) It provides a platform for real-time collaboration

c) It creates design specifications, assets, and code snippets

d) It automatically converts designs into responsive layouts

Answer: c) It creates design specifications, assets, and code snippets

Chapter 10: Photography Workflow in Lightroom

Importing, organizing, and editing photos

1. Importing Photos:

Importing is the first step in the photography workflow within Lightroom. Here's how you typically go about it:

Connect your device: Whether you're importing from a camera memory card or a folder on your computer, connect the device to your computer.

Open Lightroom: Launch Adobe Lightroom and navigate to the "Library" module, which is where the importing process takes place.

Select the source: In the Library module, click on the "Import" button or press "Ctrl + Shift + I" (Windows) or "Cmd + Shift + I" (Mac) to open the import dialog box.

Choose your photos: Browse and select the photos you want to import. You can organize them into folders during import by choosing a destination folder.

Apply presets and metadata: If you have specific presets or metadata settings you want to apply to the imported photos, you can set these in the import dialog box.

Review and import: Before hitting the "Import" button, review your selections and settings. Lightroom will then copy the photos to your designated storage location and add them to the catalog.

2. Organizing Photos:

After importing, it's crucial to organize your photos effectively to easily find and work with them:

Keywords and Metadata: Assign relevant keywords and metadata to your photos. This makes searching for specific images later much easier. Keywords can describe the subject, location, mood, and more.

Collections: Create collections to group related photos. Collections can be based on themes, projects, or any other criteria you choose. This helps in organizing photos within the catalog.

Folders and Subfolders: Organize your photos into folders and subfolders on your storage drive. This structure should mirror your desired organizational hierarchy.

Flags, Ratings, and Labels: Use flags, star ratings, and color labels to mark your best shots, categorize images, and indicate different stages of editing.

3. Editing Photos:

Lightroom provides powerful editing tools that enable you to enhance and refine your images:

Basic Adjustments: Start with basic adjustments such as exposure, contrast, highlights, shadows, whites, and blacks. These adjustments lay the foundation for your image's overall look.

Color Corrections: Adjust white balance, saturation, and vibrance to achieve accurate and visually appealing colors.

Tone Curve and HSL: Fine-tune tones and colors using the tone curve and HSL (Hue, Saturation, and Luminance) adjustments.

Sharpening and Noise Reduction: Enhance image sharpness and reduce noise to achieve a clean and crisp result.

Lens Corrections: Correct distortion, chromatic aberrations, and vignetting caused by the lens.

Local Adjustments: Use tools like the Graduated Filter, Radial Filter, and Adjustment Brush to make targeted edits to specific areas of your image.

Presets: Save your editing settings as presets to apply a consistent look to multiple images quickly.

Virtual Copies: Create virtual copies of images to experiment with different edits without affecting the original image.

Exporting: After editing, export your images in various formats and sizes for different purposes, such as sharing on social media or printing.

In Chapter 10 of the Lightroom user guide or tutorial, you will likely find detailed instructions, tips, and best practices for importing, organizing, and editing photos. Remember that an effective photography workflow is about both efficiency and creativity. By mastering these steps, you'll be able to spend more time behind the lens and less time managing your image collection.

QUIZ

Question 1: What is the first step in the photography workflow within Lightroom?

A) Editing photos

B) Exporting photos

C) Importing photos

D) Sharing photos

Answer: C) Importing photos

Question 2: Which module in Lightroom is primarily used for importing and organizing photos?

A) Develop

B) Slideshow

C) Print

D) Library

Answer: D) Library

Question 3: What is the purpose of assigning keywords and metadata to photos in Lightroom?

A) Enhancing photo resolution

B) Adding visual effects

C) Improving image exposure

D) Improving photo search and organization

Answer: D) Improving photo search and organization

Question 4: What is a collection in Lightroom?

A) A group of presets

B) A set of editing brushes

C) A way to organize photos based on themes or projects

D) A type of file format

Answer: C) A way to organize photos based on themes or projects

Question 5: Which tool in Lightroom is used to correct lens-related issues like distortion and chromatic aberration?

A) Adjustment Brush

B) Graduated Filter

C) Lens Corrections

D) Radial Filter

Answer: C) Lens Corrections

Question 6: What tool in Lightroom allows you to adjust specific areas of an image using brushes or gradients?

A) Clarity

B) HSL

C) Adjustment Brush

D) Tone Curve

Answer: C) Adjustment Brush

Question 7: What is the purpose of creating virtual copies in Lightroom?

A) To duplicate a photo without using extra storage

B) To enhance image resolution

C) To compress image files

D) To merge multiple images into one

Answer: A) To duplicate a photo without using extra storage

Applying presets and batch editing

Applying Presets:

Presets are pre-defined sets of adjustments that you can apply to your photos with a single click. They allow you to achieve a specific look, style, or mood consistently across your images. Here's how to work with presets:

Accessing Presets: In the Develop module of Lightroom, you'll find the "Presets" panel on the left side. Click on the panel to expand it and view the available presets.

Applying Presets: To apply a preset, simply click on the preset you want to use. The adjustments included in the preset will be applied to your selected photo.

Creating Your Own Presets: You can create your own presets by adjusting the various settings in the Develop module and then saving those settings as a preset. This is useful when you've developed a particular editing style you want to replicate.

Managing Presets: You can organize your presets into folders, making it easier to find the right preset for your images.

Customizing Presets: After applying a preset, you can still adjust individual settings to fine-tune the look of your photo according to your preference.

Purchasing or Downloading Presets: Many photographers and companies offer preset collections that you can purchase or download for free. These presets can be a great starting point for achieving different creative styles.

Batch Editing:

Batch editing is a technique used to apply the same set of adjustments to multiple images simultaneously. This is especially useful when you have a series of photos taken in similar lighting conditions or with consistent exposure settings. Here's how you can perform batch editing in Lightroom:

Select Multiple Photos: In the Library module, select the photos you want to edit simultaneously. You can hold down the Ctrl (Windows) or Cmd (Mac) key while clicking to select multiple photos.

Switch to Develop Module: Once your photos are selected, switch to the Develop module. Any changes you make here will be applied to all selected photos.

Apply Adjustments: Make the necessary adjustments to the first photo. This could include exposure, contrast, color adjustments, and more.

Sync Settings: After making adjustments to the first photo, go to the "Sync" button at the bottom right of the Develop module. A dialog box will appear, allowing you to choose which settings you want to sync. Check the settings you've adjusted and click "Synchronize."

Review and Refine: Lightroom will apply the adjustments to all selected photos. Review the images to ensure the adjustments look consistent across the batch. You might need to make slight adjustments to individual photos if needed.

Saving Time and Ensuring Consistency: Batch editing saves time by allowing you to apply edits to multiple images at once. It's especially useful for event photography, where you want a consistent look across a set of images.

In summary, applying presets and using batch editing are essential techniques covered in Chapter 10 of the Photography Workflow in Lightroom. These techniques enhance your efficiency and maintain a consistent style across your images, ultimately improving your overall photo editing process.

QUIZ

Question 1: What are presets in Adobe Lightroom?

A) A type of export format

B) Pre-defined sets of adjustments for photos

C) Filters that enhance image resolution

D) Folders to organize images

Answer: B) Pre-defined sets of adjustments for photos

Question 2: Which module in Lightroom is primarily used for applying presets and making adjustments to photos?

A) Import

B) Print

C) Library

D) Develop

Answer: D) Develop

Question 3: What is the purpose of applying presets to photos in Lightroom?

A) To convert photos to a different file format

B) To synchronize photos with external devices

C) To apply a consistent look or style to images

D) To organize photos into collections

Answer: C) To apply a consistent look or style to images

Question 4: What is batch editing in Lightroom?

A) Editing a single photo at a time

B) Editing photos in different software simultaneously

C) Editing photos in a series of steps

D) Editing multiple photos simultaneously with the same adjustments

Answer: D) Editing multiple photos simultaneously with the same adjustments

Question 5: How do you access the "Sync" feature in Lightroom?

A) By right-clicking on an image

B) In the Import module

C) By clicking on the "Sync" button in the Develop module

D) By selecting multiple images and pressing "Ctrl + S" (Windows) or "Cmd + S" (Mac)

Answer: C) By clicking on the "Sync" button in the Develop module

Question 6: When might batch editing be particularly useful in Lightroom?

A) When you want to edit each photo individually

B) When you have a variety of different editing styles to apply

C) When you have a set of photos taken in similar lighting conditions

D) When you want to create virtual copies of your images

Answer: C) When you have a set of photos taken in similar lighting conditions

Question 7: Can you customize adjustments after applying a preset in Lightroom?

A) No, presets are fixed and cannot be adjusted

B) Yes, adjustments can be further refined after applying a preset

C) Only if the preset is purchased from the Adobe Store

D) Only if the preset is applied in the Import module

Answer: B) Yes, adjustments can be further refined after applying a preset

Chapter 11: Adobe Dimension for 3D Design

Introduction to 3D design and visualization

Three-dimensional (3D) design and visualization have transformed the way we perceive and interact with digital content. Unlike traditional two-dimensional designs, 3D design adds depth, realism, and interactivity to visual content. This field finds application in various industries, including product design, architecture, gaming, advertising, animation, and more. One of the powerful tools in the realm of 3D design is Adobe Dimension.

Adobe Dimension:

Adobe Dimension is a versatile software tool that empowers designers to create and visualize 3D scenes and objects with ease. It bridges the gap between 2D and 3D design, allowing users to generate realistic mockups, product shots, and scenes without the need for complex 3D modeling skills. This chapter delves into the fundamentals of Adobe Dimension and its role in simplifying the 3D design process.

Key Concepts:

3D Modeling vs. 3D Visualization:

3D Modeling: This involves creating 3D objects from scratch using specialized software, requiring advanced skills in 3D geometry and sculpting. Traditional 3D modeling can be complex and time-consuming.

3D Visualization: This focuses on presenting 3D models in a realistic environment, often involving lighting, textures, and camera settings. Visualization tools like Adobe Dimension make this process more accessible to a wider range of designers.

Key Features of Adobe Dimension:

Drag-and-Drop Interface: Adobe Dimension simplifies the creation of 3D scenes by enabling users to import 2D and 3D assets via a drag-and-drop interface.

Realistic Rendering: Dimension's rendering engine generates photorealistic images, simulating lighting, shadows, reflections, and materials.

Camera and Lighting Controls: Users can adjust camera angles, depth of field, and lighting settings to achieve the desired visual impact.

Material Customization: Dimension allows users to apply and customize materials, textures, and decals to 3D objects, enhancing realism.

Integration with Adobe Creative Cloud: Dimension seamlessly integrates with other Adobe tools like Photoshop and Illustrator, allowing for easy asset exchange and collaboration.

Workflow with Adobe Dimension:

Asset Import: Start by importing 3D models, images, and graphics. Adobe Stock integration makes it easy to access a wide range of assets.

Scene Setup: Arrange and position assets within a 3D scene. Utilize the intuitive controls to adjust angles, perspectives, and camera settings.

Material Application: Apply materials and textures to your 3D objects. Customize surfaces to achieve the desired look and feel.

Lighting: Set up lighting to simulate natural or artificial illumination. Adjust shadows and reflections for added realism.

Rendering: Once the scene is set up, initiate the rendering process to generate high-quality images or interactive 3D content.

Export and Sharing: Export your creations in various formats for use in print, web, or interactive presentations. Dimension also supports 360-degree images and interactive 3D files for web display.

Conclusion:

The realm of 3D design and visualization has evolved significantly, and tools like Adobe Dimension have played a pivotal role in making this technology accessible to designers of various skill levels. By simplifying the creation of 3D scenes, Adobe Dimension empowers designers to explore new dimensions of creativity and bring their ideas to life with stunning realism. This chapter provides a foundational understanding of Adobe Dimension's capabilities and how it contributes to the broader landscape of 3D design and visualization.

QUIZ

Question 1:

What is the primary purpose of Adobe Dimension in the field of 3D design?

A) Creating complex 3D models from scratch

B) Enhancing 2D images with filters

C) Simplifying the process of 3D visualization

D) Designing 2D graphics for print

Answer: C) Simplifying the process of 3D visualization

Question 2:

Which of the following best describes 3D visualization in comparison to 3D modeling?

A) 3D visualization focuses on creating 3D objects, while 3D modeling involves realistic rendering.

B) 3D visualization involves presenting 3D models with lighting and materials, while 3D modeling involves sculpting shapes.

C) 3D visualization and 3D modeling are interchangeable terms.

D) 3D visualization involves importing 2D assets into a 3D space.

Answer: B) 3D visualization involves presenting 3D models with lighting and materials, while 3D modeling involves sculpting shapes.

Question 3:

What role does Adobe Dimension play in relation to other Adobe Creative Cloud applications?

A) It serves as a web development tool.

B) It's a video editing software.

C) It integrates seamlessly with tools like Photoshop and Illustrator for asset exchange and collaboration.

D) It's used for creating 2D vector graphics.

Answer: C) It integrates seamlessly with tools like Photoshop and Illustrator for asset exchange and collaboration.

Question 4:

Which aspect of 3D design does Adobe Dimension particularly focus on?

A) Complex mathematics for geometry manipulation

B) Realistic rendering of 3D models

C) Creating interactive virtual reality experiences

D) 2D image manipulation

Answer: B) Realistic rendering of 3D models

Question 5:

What can be achieved by adjusting camera settings in Adobe Dimension?

A) Changing the colors of the materials

B) Importing 3D models

C) Altering the background image

D) Controlling the perspective and angles of the scene

Answer: D) Controlling the perspective and angles of the scene

Question 6:

How does Adobe Dimension contribute to material customization in 3D scenes?

A) It offers pre-made 3D models that can't be customized.

B) It allows users to apply materials but doesn't support customization.

C) It enables users to apply and customize materials, textures, and decals on 3D objects.

D) It only works with 2D images and graphics.

Answer: C) It enables users to apply and customize materials, textures, and decals on 3D objects.

Question 7:

Which type of images can Adobe Dimension export for web display?

A) Only static 2D images

B) Only 3D models

C) Static 2D images and interactive 3D files

D) Animated GIFs

Answer: C) Static 2D images and interactive 3D files

Creating realistic product mockups

In the world of design and marketing, realistic product mockups are a crucial tool for presenting products in a visually appealing and convincing manner. They help businesses showcase their products in various settings and contexts, allowing potential customers to envision how these products will look and feel in real life. Adobe Dimension, a powerful 3D design and visualization tool, offers an innovative approach to creating these lifelike product mockups.

Understanding Realistic Product Mockups:

Product mockups are visual representations of products that simulate how they would appear in real-world scenarios. Traditional mockups often involved using static images of products in staged environments. However, with the advent of 3D design tools like Adobe Dimension, creating mockups has evolved into a more dynamic and immersive process.

Chapter 11: Adobe Dimension for 3D Design and Realistic Mockups:

Chapter 11 of Adobe Dimension's usage guide delves into the specific application of the tool for creating realistic product mockups. This chapter is particularly valuable for designers, marketers, and businesses aiming to elevate their product presentation strategies.

Key Steps in Creating Realistic Product Mockups with Adobe Dimension:

Asset Import:

Start by importing your product's 3D model into Adobe Dimension. If you don't have a 3D model, Adobe Dimension provides access to a library of pre-made 3D models or the ability to import 2D images as flat objects.

Scene Setup:

Arrange your product within a 3D scene. Adobe Dimension provides an intuitive interface for positioning and rotating your product in a way that aligns with your vision.

Material Application:

Apply materials, textures, and decals to your product. This step is crucial for achieving realism, as it allows you to mimic the look and feel of different materials such as wood, metal, fabric, or glass.

Lighting and Environment:

Set up lighting to replicate natural or artificial illumination. Adobe Dimension's lighting controls enable you to control shadows, reflections, and highlights to enhance the authenticity of your mockup.

Camera Settings:

Adjust the camera settings to capture your product from different angles. This allows you to showcase key features and details, giving viewers a comprehensive view of the product.

Rendering:

Initiate the rendering process to generate a high-quality image of your mockup. Adobe Dimension's rendering engine simulates realistic lighting effects, shadows, and reflections, resulting in a lifelike depiction of the product.

Post-Processing:

If necessary, you can further enhance the final image using post-processing techniques within Adobe Dimension or by exporting the image to other Adobe Creative Cloud applications.

Benefits of Using Adobe Dimension for Realistic Product Mockups:

Efficiency: Adobe Dimension streamlines the process of creating realistic mockups, reducing the need for extensive 3D modeling expertise.

Visual Realism: The software's rendering capabilities ensure that your mockups closely resemble actual product photographs, allowing customers to visualize the product accurately.

Customization: Adobe Dimension allows for easy material customization, enabling you to experiment with different textures, colors, and finishes.

Contextual Presentation: By placing products in various settings, you can communicate the product's functionality and intended use effectively.

Consistency: Adobe Dimension helps maintain consistency across mockups, ensuring that branding and product representation remain cohesive.

Conclusion:

Chapter 11 of Adobe Dimension's guide offers valuable insights into using the software to create realistic product mockups. By leveraging its intuitive tools and features, designers can produce stunning visuals that bridge the gap between imagination and reality, enabling businesses to present their products in the best possible light and make a lasting impression on their target audience.

QUIZ

Question 1:

What is the primary purpose of creating realistic product mockups?

A) To create abstract art pieces

B) To showcase 3D modeling skills

C) To present products in believable and appealing contexts

D) To simulate virtual reality experiences

Answer: C) To present products in believable and appealing contexts

Question 2:

Which software tool is highlighted in Chapter 11 for creating realistic product mockups?

A) Adobe Photoshop

B) Adobe Illustrator

C) Adobe Premiere Pro

D) Adobe Dimension

Answer: D) Adobe Dimension

Question 3:

What is a key advantage of using Adobe Dimension for creating product mockups?

A) It requires advanced 3D modeling skills.

B) It only supports 2D image editing.

C) It can only import pre-made 3D models.

D) It simplifies the process and reduces the need for extensive 3D modeling expertise.

Answer: D) It simplifies the process and reduces the need for extensive 3D modeling expertise.

Question 4:

What does the process of "material application" involve in Adobe Dimension?

A) Setting up lighting conditions

B) Adjusting camera angles

C) Applying textures, colors, and decals to 3D models

D) Exporting mockups to various formats

Answer: C) Applying textures, colors, and decals to 3D models

Question 5:

How does Adobe Dimension contribute to the realism of product mockups?

A) By providing only flat 2D images

B) By adding unrealistic effects

C) By rendering images with photorealistic lighting, shadows, and reflections

D) By making all mockups appear identical

Answer: C) By rendering images with photorealistic lighting, shadows, and reflections

Question 6:

What aspect of Adobe Dimension allows users to control how light interacts with their product mockups?

A) Material customization

B) Camera settings

C) Asset import

D) Post-processing effects

Answer: A) Material customization

Question 7:

What does adjusting camera settings in Adobe Dimension help achieve?

A) Changing the colors of the materials

B) Importing 3D models

C) Controlling the perspective and angles of the mockup

D) Altering the background image

Answer: C) Controlling the perspective and angles of the mockup

Chapter 12: Audio Editing with Adobe Audition

Basics of audio editing and mixing

In the realm of audio production, the ability to edit and mix audio is paramount to achieving professional and polished results. Adobe Audition is a powerful digital audio workstation (DAW) that provides a comprehensive set of tools for audio editing, mixing, and mastering. Chapter 12 of your reference material delves into the basics of audio editing and mixing using Adobe Audition. Let's explore the key concepts covered in this chapter:

1. Audio Editing Basics:

Importing Audio: Adobe Audition allows you to import various audio formats, such as WAV, MP3, AIFF, etc. These files appear in the "Files" panel.

Waveform Display: Audition displays audio as waveforms, which represent the amplitude of the audio signal over time. Zooming in and out allows you to work with finer details.

Selection Tools: Tools like the Selection Tool, Razor Tool, and Time Selection Tool enable you to precisely select and edit portions of audio.

Editing Operations: Cut, copy, paste, delete, fade in/out, silence, and reverse are common editing operations that help refine audio clips.

2. Multitrack Mixing:

Tracks and Clips: In the multitrack view, audio tracks represent different elements like vocals, instruments, and effects. Clips are the individual audio segments placed on these tracks.

Mixing Console: Audition's mixing console provides controls for adjusting volume, panning, EQ, and other effects for each track.

Automation: Track automation lets you create dynamic changes in parameters (volume, pan, effects) over time. This is crucial for achieving a professional mix.

Effects and Plugins: Adobe Audition offers a wide range of audio effects and plugins that enhance audio quality and creativity. These include EQ, reverb, compression, and more.

3. Editing Techniques:

Cutting and Trimming: Precisely cut unwanted sections and trim audio to remove noise, mistakes, or pauses.

Crossfades: Smoothly blend audio clips using crossfades to avoid abrupt transitions between them.

Time Stretching and Pitch Shifting: Alter the duration (time stretching) or pitch (pitch shifting) of audio clips without affecting their quality excessively.

Noise Reduction: Use tools like the Noise Reduction effect to eliminate unwanted background noise or hum.

Spectral Editing: In the spectral display, you can visualize and edit the frequency content of audio. This is useful for advanced noise removal or detailed editing.

4. Mixing Techniques:

Balancing Levels: Achieve a balanced mix by adjusting the volume levels of different tracks to ensure clarity and coherence.

Panning: Place audio elements within the stereo field using panning to create a sense of space and separation.

Equalization (EQ): Shape the tonal balance of tracks by boosting or cutting specific frequencies.

Compression: Control the dynamic range of audio by reducing loud peaks and boosting quieter sections.

Reverb and Effects: Apply reverb to simulate different acoustic spaces and experiment with other effects to add depth and character.

5. Mastering:

Final Touches: Mastering involves fine-tuning the overall mix for optimal playback on different systems. This includes adjustments to EQ, compression, and limiting.

Exporting: Once the mix and mastering are complete, you can export the final audio file in various formats suitable for distribution or playback.

In conclusion, Adobe Audition is a versatile tool that empowers audio professionals to edit and mix audio with precision and creativity. The basics of audio editing and mixing covered in Chapter 12 provide a solid foundation for anyone looking to produce high-quality audio content. By understanding these concepts and practicing with Audition's features, you can craft polished and captivating audio productions.

QUIZ

Question 1:

Which tool in Adobe Audition allows you to select and edit specific portions of an audio clip precisely?

a) Razor Tool

b) Volume Tool

c) Pan Tool

d) Play Tool

Answer: a) Razor Tool

Question 2:

What does the term "crossfade" refer to in audio editing?

a) Enhancing bass frequencies

b) Blending audio clips smoothly

c) Amplifying the volume abruptly

d) Changing the pitch of audio

Answer: b) Blending audio clips smoothly

Question 3:

What is the purpose of track automation in audio mixing?

a) Creating new audio tracks

b) Adjusting the sample rate of tracks

c) Applying effects to tracks

d) Modifying parameters over time

Answer: d) Modifying parameters over time

Question 4:

Which audio editing technique involves adjusting the duration of an audio clip without significantly affecting its quality?

a) Pitch shifting

b) Crossfading

c) Time stretching

d) Spectral editing

Answer: c) Time stretching

Question 5:

Which audio effect is commonly used to reduce unwanted background noise or hum from recordings?

a) Reverb

b) Compression

c) Equalization

d) Noise Reduction

Answer: d) Noise Reduction

Question 6:

What is the purpose of panning in audio mixing?

a) Adjusting the overall volume of a track

b) Enhancing the bass frequencies of a track

c) Placing audio elements within the stereo field

d) Applying reverb to a track

Answer: c) Placing audio elements within the stereo field

Question 7:

Which step of audio production involves fine-tuning the overall mix for optimal playback on different systems?

a) Noise Reduction

b) Equalization

c) Mixing

d) Mastering

Answer: d) Mastering

Question 8:

Which Adobe Audition tool allows you to visualize and edit the frequency content of audio?

a) Razor Tool

b) Time Selection Tool

c) Spectral Display

d) Crossfade Tool

Answer: c) Spectral Display

Question 9:

Which audio effect is used to control the dynamic range of audio by reducing loud peaks and boosting quieter sections?

a) Reverb

b) Compression

c) Equalization

d) Delay

Answer: b) Compression

Question 10:

What is the main purpose of exporting audio in Adobe Audition?

a) Adjusting volume levels

b) Applying special effects

c) Preparing audio for distribution or playback

d) Mixing multiple audio tracks

Answer: c) Preparing audio for distribution or playback

Podcast production and sound restoration

In the digital age, podcasts have emerged as a popular form of content delivery, offering listeners a wide range of topics and discussions. Producing a high-quality podcast involves not only engaging content but also clear and professional audio. Chapter 12 of your reference material covers podcast production and sound restoration using Adobe Audition. Let's delve into the key concepts discussed in this chapter:

1. Podcast Production:

Recording Setup: A quality podcast begins with a good recording setup. A microphone, pop filter, headphones, and a quiet recording environment are essential.

Recording Techniques: Ensure consistent microphone placement, maintain a consistent vocal distance, and avoid excessive background noise during recording.

Editing for Clarity: Adobe Audition's editing tools allow you to cut out mistakes, pauses, or distractions, creating a seamless flow in your podcast.

Adding Intro and Outro: Incorporate an engaging introduction and a memorable outro to give your podcast a professional touch.

2. Sound Restoration:

Noise Reduction: Adobe Audition provides tools like Noise Reduction to remove unwanted background noise, hum, or hiss from your recordings.

De-essing: Address harsh "s" and "sh" sounds using de-essing tools to create a smoother listening experience.

Spectral Frequency Display: The spectral display in Audition enables you to visualize and edit specific frequencies, making it useful for precise noise removal.

Restoring Old Recordings: For historical or archival content, you can use tools to restore and enhance older recordings that may have deteriorated over time.

3. Voice Enhancement:

Equalization (EQ): Adjust the frequency balance of voices to enhance clarity and presence. Boosting or cutting specific frequencies can improve the overall sound.

Compression: Apply compression to even out vocal dynamics, ensuring that softer parts are audible and louder parts are controlled.

De-clip and De-click: These tools help repair audio that might have clipping distortion or clicking artifacts, ensuring a cleaner sound.

4. Mixing and Mastering:

Balancing Multiple Voices: In podcasts with multiple hosts or guests, use the mixing console to balance their voices and ensure they are all audible and clear.

Leveling and Automation: Apply automation to adjust volume levels over time, ensuring a consistent listening experience.

Mastering for Podcasts: Mastering involves optimizing the final mix for various listening environments and devices, enhancing overall loudness and dynamics.

5. Exporting and Distribution:

Export Settings: Choose appropriate export settings based on podcast distribution platforms and desired audio quality. Common formats include MP3 and AAC.

Metadata and Tagging: Add metadata such as episode title, show notes, and cover art to enhance the professionalism of your podcast.

Uploading to Platforms: Distribute your podcast to platforms like Apple Podcasts, Spotify, Google Podcasts, and more, making it accessible to a wider audience.

In conclusion, Chapter 12 of your reference material covers podcast production and sound restoration using Adobe Audition. Podcast production involves careful recording techniques, editing for clarity, and enhancing the overall sound quality. Sound restoration tools in Audition allow you to improve audio quality by removing noise, addressing frequency issues, and enhancing voice recordings. With the help of Adobe Audition's features and techniques outlined in this chapter, you can create engaging, professional-sounding podcasts that captivate and retain your audience's attention.

QUIZ

Question 1:

What is a key consideration for achieving quality podcast recordings?

a) Using any available microphone

b) Recording in a noisy environment

c) Having a quiet recording space

d) Recording without headphones

Answer: c) Having a quiet recording space

Question 2:

Which Adobe Audition tool can be used to remove unwanted background noise or hum from podcast recordings?

a) Spectral Frequency Display

b) Volume Envelope

c) Pitch Shifter

d) Pan Tool

Answer: a) Spectral Frequency Display

Question 3:

What is the purpose of using de-essing in podcast production?

a) Enhancing bass frequencies

b) Removing background noise

c) Addressing harsh vocal sounds

d) Adding reverb to vocals

Answer: c) Addressing harsh vocal sounds

Question 4:

Which audio editing technique involves applying compression to ensure even vocal dynamics in a podcast episode?

a) Noise Reduction

b) Time Stretching

c) Crossfading

d) Compression

Answer: d) Compression

Question 5:

What is the purpose of mastering in podcast production?

a) Removing unwanted noises

b) Adjusting volume levels during recording

c) Preparing the final mix for distribution

d) Enhancing vocal clarity

Answer: c) Preparing the final mix for distribution

Question 6:

What does the term "metadata" refer to in podcast production?

a) Unwanted background noise

b) Editing techniques in Audition

c) Episode titles and show notes

d) Spectral display visualization

Answer: c) Episode titles and show notes

Question 7:

What role does the mixing console play in podcast production?

a) Applying noise reduction

b) Enhancing vocal EQ

c) Adjusting volume levels and effects

d) Removing clicks and pops

Answer: c) Adjusting volume levels and effects

Question 8:

Which tool in Adobe Audition can visualize and edit the frequency content of audio for precise noise removal?

a) Pan Tool

b) Time Selection Tool

c) Spectral Frequency Display

d) Volume Envelope

Answer: c) Spectral Frequency Display

Question 9:

What does "de-clip" in audio restoration refer to?

a) Applying reverb to audio

b) Reducing background noise

c) Addressing harsh vocal sounds

d) Repairing clipped audio recordings

Answer: d) Repairing clipped audio recordings

Question 10:

What type of audio artifact can "de-click" tools in Adobe Audition help to repair?

a) Background noise

b) Hiss and hum

c) Harsh vocal sounds

d) Clicking noises or artifacts

Answer: d) Clicking noises or artifacts

Chapter 13: Adobe Spark for Quick Content Creation

Creating social media graphics, web pages, and videos

Adobe Spark is a user-friendly content creation tool that allows individuals and businesses to create engaging visuals, web pages, and videos without the need for extensive design or technical skills. It's designed to streamline the content creation process and provide a variety of templates, customization options, and tools to make your content stand out on social media and the web.

Creating Social Media Graphics:

Choose a Platform: Adobe Spark offers templates for various social media platforms like Instagram, Facebook, Twitter, and more. Select the platform you want to create content for.

Select a Template: Browse through the available templates for social media graphics. These templates are pre-designed with different layouts, fonts, colors, and placeholders for images and text.

Customization: Customize the template by adding your own images, text, and branding elements. You can change colors, fonts, and layout to match your brand's aesthetic.

Visual Enhancements: Adobe Spark provides tools to enhance your images, including filters, overlays, and effects. You can also add icons, stickers, and other design elements to make your graphics more visually appealing.

Text and Typography: Add text to convey your message. Experiment with different fonts, sizes, and alignments to ensure readability. You can also animate text for dynamic effects.

Exporting: Once you're satisfied with your design, export it in the appropriate format for your chosen social media platform. Adobe Spark often offers optimized sizes for different platforms.

Creating Web Pages:

Start a Project: In Adobe Spark, select the option to create a web page. Choose a template that suits your content's purpose, such as an event announcement, portfolio, or blog post.

Layout and Content: Customize the layout by adding sections, images, videos, and text. The drag-and-drop interface makes it easy to arrange elements and experiment with different designs.

Text and Headings: Craft engaging and informative content using text and headings. Use a combination of fonts, font sizes, and colors to make your content visually appealing and easy to read.

Media Integration: Embed images and videos directly into your web page. Adobe Spark allows you to upload your own media or search for relevant content from platforms like Unsplash and Adobe Stock.

Links and Buttons: Create interactive elements like buttons and links to direct visitors to other pages, external websites, or social media profiles.

Preview and Publish: Preview your web page to ensure everything looks as intended. Once you're satisfied, publish it. Adobe Spark provides a shareable link that you can distribute through various channels.

Creating Videos:

Choose a Template: Adobe Spark offers video templates for different purposes, such as promotional videos, tutorials, and event recaps.

Storyboarding: Plan your video's structure by adding scenes. Each scene can contain text, images, videos, and transitions.

Media Import: Upload your own videos and images, or use stock media available within Adobe Spark. Arrange these elements in the desired sequence.

Transitions and Effects: Add transitions between scenes for smooth visual flow. Apply effects like filters and animations to enhance your video's appeal.

Text and Narration: Overlay text to provide context, explanations, or captions. You can also record narration directly within Adobe Spark or upload an audio file.

Music and Sound: Choose from a library of royalty-free music or upload your own audio tracks to complement your video.

Preview and Export: Preview your video to ensure everything looks and sounds right. Once satisfied, export the video in your preferred resolution. Adobe Spark often provides options optimized for social media, web, or presentations.

Remember that Adobe Spark offers a balance between simplicity and creativity, making it an excellent tool for quick content creation across social media graphics, web pages, and videos. While my knowledge is up to September 2021, you should explore Adobe Spark's official resources for the most up-to-date information and features.

QUIZ

Question 1: Which Adobe tool is specifically designed for quick content creation, offering templates and customization options for social media graphics, web pages, and videos?

a) Adobe Photoshop

b) Adobe Illustrator

c) Adobe Spark

d) Adobe InDesign

Answer: c) Adobe Spark

Question 2: When creating social media graphics using Adobe Spark, what can you customize in the templates to match your brand's aesthetic?

a) Template size only

b) Fonts and layout only

c) Colors, fonts, and layout

d) Images and videos only

Answer: c) Colors, fonts, and layout

Question 3: In Adobe Spark, what type of elements can you add to enhance your social media graphics, such as stickers, overlays, and effects?

a) Animations

b) Filters

c) Background music

d) Interactive buttons

Answer: b) Filters

Question 4: Which step involves embedding images, videos, and text sections into a web page created using Adobe Spark?

a) Adding filters

b) Customizing layout

c) Applying transitions

d) Previewing the design

Answer: b) Customizing layout

Question 5: In Adobe Spark, what type of content can you include in a video's storyboard for different scenes?

a) Only text elements

b) Only images

c) Only videos

d) Text, images, videos, and transitions

Answer: d) Text, images, videos, and transitions

Question 6: What can you use to create interactive elements like buttons and links within your Adobe Spark web page?

a) Only text elements

b) Only images

c) Only videos

d) Text, images, and videos

Answer: d) Text, images, and videos

Question 7: Which feature in Adobe Spark allows you to add narration to your videos directly within the platform?

a) Media Import

b) Text Overlay

c) Transitions

d) Audio Recording

Answer: d) Audio Recording

Using templates and customization options

Using Templates and Customization Options in Adobe Spark

Adobe Spark simplifies the content creation process by offering a wide range of templates and customization options for creating social media graphics, web pages, and videos. These templates provide a foundation for your projects, allowing you to save time while maintaining a professional and visually appealing design. Here's how you can effectively use templates and customize them to suit your needs:

1. Selecting the Right Template:

When you start a new project in Adobe Spark, you'll be prompted to choose a template based on the type of content you're creating. For instance, if you're creating a social media graphic, you'll find templates tailored to platforms like Instagram, Facebook, and Twitter. If you're working on a web page, you'll find templates for different purposes like portfolios, announcements, and more. Video templates cater to various styles such as tutorials, event recaps, and promotions.

2. Template Features:

Templates in Adobe Spark come with a variety of pre-designed features, including:

Layout: Templates have predefined layouts that determine where images, text, and other elements will be placed on the canvas.

Typography: Fonts, font sizes, and font styles are often preset in templates to ensure consistency and readability.

Colors: Templates include color schemes that you can either stick with or customize to match your brand's color palette.

Graphics: Placeholder images and design elements are often included in templates, giving you a starting point for visual content.

3. Customizing Templates:

While templates provide a foundation, it's important to customize them to make your content unique and aligned with your brand's identity:

Images and Videos: Replace the placeholder images and videos with your own content. You can upload media from your device or choose from Adobe Spark's library of stock images and videos.

Text: Edit the text elements to convey your message. You can change headings, subheadings, captions, and more. Consider using text to highlight key points and engage your audience.

Colors: Customize the color scheme to match your branding. Consistent colors create a cohesive look across your content.

Typography: Adjust font styles, sizes, and alignments to enhance the visual appeal and readability of your content.

Layout: While templates provide a layout structure, you can rearrange and resize elements as needed to create a unique composition.

Additional Elements: Add icons, stickers, overlays, and other graphic elements to further enhance your content's visual impact.

4. Preview and Feedback:

Before finalizing your content, use Adobe Spark's preview feature to see how your customized template looks. This is a great time to gather feedback from colleagues, friends, or clients to ensure your content effectively communicates your message.

5. Publish and Share:

Once you're satisfied with your customization, you can publish your content directly from Adobe Spark. Social media graphics can be shared on their respective platforms, web pages can be shared via links, and videos can be exported in various formats for sharing online.

Benefits of Using Templates and Customization:

Time Efficiency: Templates eliminate the need to start from scratch, saving you time in the design process.

Consistency: Templates help maintain a consistent look and feel across your content.

Professionalism: Even if you're not a design expert, templates ensure your content has a polished appearance.

Branding: Customization options allow you to incorporate your brand's visual elements into the content.

Creativity: While templates provide structure, you have the creative freedom to make your content unique.

In conclusion, using templates and customization options in Adobe Spark streamlines the content creation process, allowing you to create engaging social media graphics, web pages, and videos with ease. By selecting the right template and effectively customizing it to match your needs, you can create impactful content that resonates with your target audience.

QUIZ

Question 1: What is the primary benefit of using templates in Adobe Spark for content creation?

a) They require advanced design skills.

b) They limit creative freedom.

c) They save time and provide a foundation for design.

d) They only work for social media graphics.

Answer: c) They save time and provide a foundation for design.

Question 2: What types of content can be created using templates in Adobe Spark?

a) Only social media graphics

b) Only web pages

c) Only videos

d) Social media graphics, web pages, and videos

Answer: d) Social media graphics, web pages, and videos

Question 3: What does the term "customization" refer to when using templates in Adobe Spark?

a) Replacing all template elements with new ones

b) Changing the color scheme only

c) Making minor adjustments to template elements to suit your needs

d) Adding more templates to the project

Answer: c) Making minor adjustments to template elements to suit your needs

Question 4: Which of the following can be customized in Adobe Spark templates to match your brand's identity?

a) Template structure only

b) Font styles and sizes only

c) Colors, typography, layout, and imagery

d) Only the provided placeholder text

Answer: c) Colors, typography, layout, and imagery

Question 5: How does customization impact the overall look of your content created using Adobe Spark templates?

a) Customization erases the template's design entirely.

b) Customization has no effect on the design elements.

c) Customization improves the design by making it more consistent.

d) Customization often degrades the design quality.

Answer: c) Customization improves the design by making it more consistent.

Question 6: Which Adobe Spark feature allows you to replace placeholder images and videos with your own media?

a) Typography customization

b) Media import

c) Animation tools

d) Audio recording

Answer: b) Media import

Question 7: What is the purpose of using Adobe Spark's preview feature after customizing a template?

a) To share the content on social media platforms

b) To apply filters to the design

c) To gather feedback and ensure the content looks as intended

d) To automatically publish the content

Answer: c) To gather feedback and ensure the content looks as intended

Chapter 14: Collaboration and Productivity Tools

Sharing files and collaborating with Creative Cloud Libraries

Adobe Creative Cloud Libraries is a feature-rich platform that enables creative professionals to share and collaborate on design assets, files, and projects seamlessly. It's integrated with popular Adobe software such as Photoshop, Illustrator, InDesign, and others, making it easy to access and manage shared content across applications.

Key Features:

Centralized Asset Repository: Creative Cloud Libraries act as a centralized repository for all design assets, including images, graphics, color palettes, character styles, and more. These assets are stored in the cloud, making them accessible from any device with an internet connection.

Cross-Application Integration: Libraries are integrated into various Adobe applications, allowing users to access shared assets directly from the software they're working in. This integration streamlines the creative process, eliminating the need to switch between applications to find the required assets.

Collaboration and Sharing: Creative Cloud Libraries facilitate collaboration by allowing multiple users to work on the same project simultaneously. Designers can create libraries and invite team members to collaborate, share, and contribute to the assets within. Permissions can be set to control who can edit or view assets.

Version Control: Libraries offer version control capabilities, ensuring that users can keep track of changes made to assets over time. This feature is especially valuable in creative projects where multiple iterations and modifications are common.

Syncing Across Devices: Creative Cloud Libraries sync seamlessly across devices. This means that any changes made to an asset on one device are automatically reflected on all devices with access to the library. This feature enhances flexibility and allows designers to continue their work from different locations.

Search and Filter: Libraries provide robust search and filtering options, making it easy to find specific assets within a large collection. This feature improves efficiency and reduces the time spent searching for the right element.

Offline Access: While Creative Cloud Libraries primarily rely on cloud storage, Adobe applications allow users to make certain library assets available offline. This feature ensures that users can continue working even without an internet connection.

Workflow Using Creative Cloud Libraries:

Creating Libraries: A designer initiates the process by creating a library within the Adobe Creative Cloud platform. The library can be named and categorized according to the project or asset type.

Adding Assets: Designers can add a wide range of assets to the library, including images, graphics, text styles, color swatches, and more. These assets can be created within Adobe software or imported from external sources.

Inviting Collaborators: Once the library is populated with assets, designers can invite team members or collaborators to join. Collaborators receive invitations and, upon acceptance, gain access to the library.

Collaboration and Editing: Collaborators can edit, modify, or reuse assets within the library. They can also contribute new assets to the library, fostering a collaborative and iterative creative process.

Application Integration: When working in Adobe applications like Photoshop or Illustrator, designers can access library assets directly from the application's interface. This eliminates the need to switch between software to access the required assets.

Syncing and Version Control: As assets are used, edited, or updated, the changes are automatically synced across devices and applications. The version control feature ensures that users can track changes and revert to previous versions if needed.

Project Completion: Once the project is completed, the final versions of the assets are stored in the library. These assets can be reused in future projects or shared with clients and stakeholders.

In conclusion, Creative Cloud Libraries play a significant role in streamlining collaboration and file sharing within creative teams. Their integration with Adobe applications, version control capabilities, and seamless syncing across devices make them essential tools for modern designers. By providing a centralized repository for design assets and fostering collaboration, Creative Cloud Libraries contribute to enhanced productivity and efficiency in creative projects.

QUIZ

What is the main purpose of Adobe Creative Cloud Libraries?

a) A cloud-based word processing tool

b) A social media platform for creatives

c) A repository for sharing and collaborating on design assets

d) A video editing software

Answer: c) A repository for sharing and collaborating on design assets

What type of assets can be stored in Creative Cloud Libraries?

a) Only text documents

b) Only images

c) Images, graphics, color palettes, character styles, and more

d) Only audio files

Answer: c) Images, graphics, color palettes, character styles, and more

How does Creative Cloud Libraries support collaboration among team members?

a) By allowing only one person to edit assets at a time

b) By enabling real-time collaborative editing of assets

c) By restricting access to assets to prevent collaboration

d) By limiting the number of assets that can be shared

Answer: b) By enabling real-time collaborative editing of assets

Which of the following is a benefit of using Creative Cloud Libraries in terms of version control?

a) It automatically deletes previous versions of assets

b) It allows collaborators to make changes without tracking versions

c) It keeps track of changes made to assets over time

d) It prevents collaborators from making any changes to assets

Answer: c) It keeps track of changes made to assets over time

What is the advantage of Creative Cloud Libraries syncing across devices?

a) It can only be accessed on one designated device

b) It allows offline access only

c) Changes made on one device are automatically reflected on all devices

d) It only works on desktop computers, not on mobile devices

Answer: c) Changes made on one device are automatically reflected on all devices

How can designers access assets from Creative Cloud Libraries while working in Adobe applications?

a) By using a separate web browser to access the library

b) By manually copying and pasting the assets into the application

c) By accessing the assets directly from the application's interface

d) By downloading the assets and then importing them into the application

Answer: c) By accessing the assets directly from the application's interface

What type of assets can be made available offline in Creative Cloud Libraries?

a) Only text styles

b) Only color palettes

c) All assets stored in the library

d) None of the assets can be made available offline

Answer: c) All assets stored in the library

Using Adobe Fonts and Stock for creative assets

Adobe Fonts and Adobe Stock are two integral components of Adobe's creative ecosystem that provide designers with a wide range of high-quality fonts and stock assets, respectively. These tools streamline the process of finding, licensing, and incorporating assets into creative projects.

Adobe Fonts:

Adobe Fonts, previously known as Typekit, offers an extensive collection of fonts that can be easily integrated into various design applications. Here's how it contributes to collaboration and productivity:

Access to High-Quality Fonts: Adobe Fonts provides access to a diverse library of typefaces designed by renowned foundries and designers. Designers can choose from a wide range of styles, from classic to modern, ensuring that they find the perfect font for their project's tone and message.

Synchronized Fonts: Adobe Fonts seamlessly integrates with Adobe Creative Cloud applications. Designers can activate fonts from the library, and they automatically sync across different devices, ensuring consistency in design across platforms.

Collaboration with Consistency: When working collaboratively, the ability to sync fonts across devices ensures that all team members are using the same fonts. This enhances consistency in design and prevents compatibility issues.

Easy Activation: Adobe Fonts can be activated with a single click, eliminating the need for manual font installations. This makes it easy for collaborators to access and use specific fonts without any technical hurdles.

Preview and Experimentation: Designers can preview fonts directly within the Adobe software interface before making a selection. This feature aids in experimentation and allows designers to make informed font choices.

Adobe Stock:

Adobe Stock provides a vast collection of royalty-free images, videos, illustrations, and templates that can be used in various creative projects. Its integration with Adobe Creative Cloud applications simplifies the process of finding and incorporating assets into projects:

Comprehensive Asset Library: Adobe Stock offers a diverse library of assets, including photos, graphics, videos, and templates. Designers can search for assets based on keywords, themes, colors, and more.

Streamlined Licensing: Adobe Stock assets come with integrated licensing, ensuring that designers have the legal right to use the assets in their projects. This simplifies the legal aspects of using third-party assets.

Direct Integration: Adobe Stock is directly integrated into Adobe Creative Cloud applications. Designers can search for and license assets without leaving their workspace, reducing the need to switch between applications.

Creative Flexibility: The availability of high-quality assets from Adobe Stock empowers designers to quickly find suitable visuals for their projects. This speeds up the creative process and enhances productivity.

Collaborative Workflows: When collaborating on projects, team members can access the same Adobe Stock assets within the Adobe software, ensuring that everyone is using the same visuals.

Workflow Using Adobe Fonts and Adobe Stock:

Accessing Libraries: Designers access the Adobe Fonts and Adobe Stock libraries through their Adobe Creative Cloud accounts.

Browsing and Selection: For fonts, designers browse through the Adobe Fonts library, previewing and selecting fonts that suit their project's requirements. For assets, designers search for specific images, videos, or templates within Adobe Stock based on project needs.

Integration: Chosen fonts are automatically synced across Adobe applications, while Adobe Stock assets can be directly integrated into projects using the Creative Cloud libraries or panels.

Collaboration: Collaborators can access the same fonts and Adobe Stock assets if they have access to the same Adobe Creative Cloud account or shared libraries, ensuring consistency in design.

Project Completion: The selected fonts and assets contribute to the creative project's design and visual elements, enhancing the overall quality and aesthetics of the final deliverables.

In conclusion, Adobe Fonts and Adobe Stock are valuable tools within Adobe's suite of applications that significantly enhance collaboration and productivity in creative workflows. By providing a vast array of fonts and assets directly integrated into the design software, designers can easily access, experiment with, and incorporate high-quality elements into their projects, leading to more efficient and visually appealing outcomes.

QUIZ

What is the primary purpose of Adobe Fonts?

a) A tool for creating vector illustrations

b) A platform for sharing design files with clients

c) A collection of high-quality fonts for creative projects

d) A video editing software

Answer: c) A collection of high-quality fonts for creative projects

What advantage does Adobe Fonts offer in terms of collaboration?

a) It allows direct integration with social media platforms

b) It provides a comprehensive library of stock images

c) It offers real-time collaborative editing of fonts

d) It syncs fonts across devices for consistent design among collaborators

Answer: d) It syncs fonts across devices for consistent design among collaborators

What type of assets can be found on Adobe Stock?

a) Only fonts

b) Only vector graphics

c) Royalty-free images, videos, illustrations, and templates

d) Only audio files

Answer: c) Royalty-free images, videos, illustrations, and templates

How does Adobe Stock simplify the licensing process for its assets?

a) It doesn't require any licensing for its assets

b) It automatically generates licenses for each project

c) It provides assets without any restrictions

d) It includes integrated licensing for hassle-free use of assets

Answer: d) It includes integrated licensing for hassle-free use of assets

What is the advantage of Adobe Stock's integration with Adobe Creative Cloud applications?

a) It offers a standalone interface for asset management

b) It limits access to Adobe Stock assets to only one device

c) It allows assets to be downloaded and imported manually

d) It enables direct access and integration of assets within the creative software interface

Answer: d) It enables direct access and integration of assets within the creative software interface

How can designers preview fonts from Adobe Fonts before using them in their projects?

a) By downloading and installing the fonts on their device

b) By searching for fonts using external web browsers

c) By previewing fonts directly within the Adobe software interface

d) By requesting font samples from Adobe customer support

Answer: c) By previewing fonts directly within the Adobe software interface

Why is using Adobe Fonts and Adobe Stock advantageous for collaboration in creative projects?

a) They offer real-time project management features

b) They provide an exclusive platform for designers to showcase their work

c) They eliminate the need for collaboration by automating design tasks

d) They offer access to a variety of fonts and assets, ensuring consistent design and visual elements among collaborators

Answer: d) They offer access to a variety of fonts and assets, ensuring consistent design and visual elements among collaborators

Chapter 15: Workflows and Integration

Seamless integration between Creative Cloud apps

In the context of Adobe Creative Cloud, workflows and integration refer to the smooth and efficient collaboration and interaction between different software applications within the Creative Cloud suite. Adobe has designed its suite of creative tools with the idea that professionals often work on multiple aspects of a project, such as graphic design, photo editing, video production, and web development. Seamless integration between these tools streamlines the creative process and allows users to move content between applications without losing fidelity, ensuring a consistent and coherent result.

Key Concepts and Features:

Shared Assets and Libraries: Adobe Creative Cloud apps often allow users to create and manage shared assets, such as graphics, logos, and styles. These assets can be stored in shared libraries, accessible across different applications. This feature ensures consistency in design elements and branding throughout various projects.

Dynamic Linking (Video and Animation): In video production and animation workflows, dynamic linking allows for real-time updates between Adobe Premiere Pro, After Effects, and other applications. Changes made in one application are automatically reflected in another, eliminating the need to export and import files repeatedly.

Smart Objects (Photoshop and Illustrator): Smart Objects maintain the quality and flexibility of raster and vector graphics across applications. Users can create a Smart Object in one application and easily edit it in another without losing resolution or editability.

Direct Integration with Adobe Stock: Creative Cloud apps offer direct integration with Adobe Stock, allowing users to search for and license high-quality assets without leaving their current application. This integration streamlines the process of finding images, videos, and other resources.

Cross-Application Compatibility: Adobe has designed its applications to work harmoniously together. For instance, a designer can create vector graphics in Adobe Illustrator and then import them seamlessly into Adobe InDesign for layout design.

Workflow Presets and Profiles: Users can save their preferred settings and configurations as presets or profiles. These settings can be shared across applications, ensuring consistency in color profiles, typography, and other design aspects.

Plugins and Extensions: Adobe Creative Cloud apps support third-party plugins and extensions that enhance functionality and add new features. These extensions can provide specialized tools for specific tasks, expanding the capabilities of the software suite.

Cloud-Based Storage and Collaboration: Adobe Creative Cloud offers cloud-based storage that allows users to save their projects and assets online. This enables collaboration between team members, as multiple users can access, edit, and comment on shared projects from different locations.

Benefits:

Seamless integration between Creative Cloud apps offers several benefits:

Efficiency: Designers and creatives can transition between different applications smoothly, minimizing the need for manual file conversions and optimizations.

Consistency: Design elements, such as colors, fonts, and styles, can be maintained consistently throughout different projects.

Time Savings: Integration eliminates repetitive tasks like exporting and importing files, saving valuable time during the creative process.

Collaboration: Multiple team members can work on different aspects of a project using their preferred Creative Cloud apps, all while sharing and collaborating on assets through cloud storage.

Flexibility: Creatives can leverage the strengths of different applications for specific tasks, ensuring the best results for each aspect of their project.

In conclusion, seamless integration between Adobe Creative Cloud apps is a crucial aspect of modern creative workflows. It allows professionals to leverage the strengths of different applications while maintaining consistency and efficiency throughout their projects. This integration streamlines collaboration, enhances productivity, and empowers creatives to bring their visions to life. While the details of Chapter 15 may provide additional insights, the core concepts of integration discussed here remain central to the Adobe Creative Cloud ecosystem.

QUIZ

What is the primary benefit of seamless integration between Creative Cloud apps?

a) Access to Adobe Stock images

b) Improved computer performance

c) Consistency in design elements

d) Enhanced touch screen support

Answer: c) Consistency in design elements

Which feature allows real-time updates between Adobe Premiere Pro and After Effects?

a) Cloud-based storage

b) Dynamic Linking

c) Smart Objects

d) Photoshop Libraries

Answer: b) Dynamic Linking

Which Adobe Creative Cloud feature enables users to share graphics, logos, and styles across different applications?

a) Smart Objects

b) Adobe Stock integration

c) Dynamic Linking

d) Shared Libraries

Answer: d) Shared Libraries

What is the advantage of using workflow presets and profiles in Creative Cloud apps?

a) They automatically save files to the cloud

b) They enhance touch screen support

c) They enable real-time collaboration

d) They ensure consistency in settings and configurations

Answer: d) They ensure consistency in settings and configurations

Which Adobe Creative Cloud feature allows users to import vector graphics from Illustrator into InDesign without losing quality?

a) Dynamic Linking

b) Smart Objects

c) Plugins and Extensions

d) Shared Libraries

Answer: b) Smart Objects

What is the main purpose of using plugins and extensions in Adobe Creative Cloud apps?

a) Enhance cloud storage capabilities

b) Streamline asset licensing

c) Extend the functionality of the software

d) Enable cross-device synchronization

Answer: c) Extend the functionality of the software

How does cloud-based storage facilitate collaboration in Creative Cloud workflows?

a) It enables direct integration with Adobe Stock

b) It automatically converts files between formats

c) It allows users to save files to local drives

d) It allows multiple users to access, edit, and share projects from different locations

Answer: d) It allows multiple users to access, edit, and share projects from different locations

What does "seamless integration" between Creative Cloud apps mean?

a) The ability to use apps without an internet connection

b) The automatic synchronization of files across devices

c) The smooth interaction and sharing of content between different Adobe apps

d) The ability to work on projects without using any plugins

Answer: c) The smooth interaction and sharing of content between different Adobe apps

Which feature of Adobe Creative Cloud apps allows users to search for and license assets without leaving their current application?

a) Smart Objects

b) Dynamic Linking

c) Shared Libraries

d) Adobe Stock integration

Answer: d) Adobe Stock integration

What's the benefit of using shared libraries in Adobe Creative Cloud?

a) They automatically save your files to the cloud

b) They allow you to edit files directly in the browser

c) They ensure consistent design elements across different projects and apps

d) They provide real-time collaboration tools

Answer: c) They ensure consistent design elements across different projects and apps

Leveraging Adobe Bridge for asset management

Adobe Bridge is a digital asset management tool that acts as a hub for managing, organizing, and accessing various types of media assets, including images, videos, audio files, and documents. While not a creative application itself, Adobe Bridge plays a vital role in streamlining workflows by providing a central platform for asset organization and integration.

Key Features of Adobe Bridge:

Asset Organization: Adobe Bridge allows users to organize assets using folders, collections, and keywords. This structured approach simplifies asset retrieval and ensures that files are easily accessible when needed.

Metadata Management: Users can assign metadata such as keywords, descriptions, and copyright information to assets. This metadata helps in searching and categorizing assets effectively.

Preview and Review: Adobe Bridge provides visual previews of various file types, allowing users to quickly review images, videos, and documents without opening separate applications.

Batch Renaming and Batch Processing: Users can perform batch renaming and apply batch edits to multiple files simultaneously, saving time and effort.

Integration with Creative Cloud Apps: Adobe Bridge seamlessly integrates with other Creative Cloud applications, allowing users to open assets directly in applications like Photoshop, Illustrator, and InDesign. This integration eliminates the need to navigate through folders to find the desired file.

Adobe Stock Integration: Adobe Bridge provides access to Adobe Stock directly from the application, making it easier to license and download assets for use in projects.

Cross-Platform Compatibility: Adobe Bridge is available on both Windows and macOS platforms, ensuring compatibility across different operating systems.

Relevance to Workflows and Integration:

In the context of Chapter 15, leveraging Adobe Bridge for asset management is essential for optimizing workflows and integration within the Creative Cloud suite:

Centralized Asset Repository: Adobe Bridge serves as a centralized repository for assets, making it convenient to locate and manage files for different projects. This centralized approach enhances collaboration by allowing team members to access and use assets efficiently.

Efficient Integration: By connecting Adobe Bridge with other Creative Cloud applications, designers and creatives can seamlessly transition between asset management and content creation without disruptions.

Consistency and Collaboration: Adobe Bridge's features like metadata management and keyword tagging enable users to maintain consistency in asset organization. This consistency is particularly valuable in collaborative settings where multiple team members need to access and contribute to projects.

Simplified Review Processes: The ability to preview assets without opening separate applications facilitates the review process, allowing stakeholders to quickly assess the suitability of assets for a project.

Streamlined Editing: Adobe Bridge's integration with Creative Cloud apps enables users to directly open assets in their preferred applications, streamlining the editing process.

Time and Resource Savings: Batch processing and batch renaming features help users save time and effort when handling large numbers of assets, contributing to overall workflow efficiency.

In conclusion, leveraging Adobe Bridge for asset management aligns with the themes of workflows and integration discussed in Chapter 15. The tool's capabilities, such as asset organization, metadata management, and integration with Creative Cloud apps, contribute to smoother workflows, efficient collaboration, and effective utilization of media assets throughout the creative process.

QUIZ

What is the primary purpose of Adobe Bridge in the context of creative workflows?

a) Video editing

b) Asset management

c) 3D modeling

d) Web development

Answer: b) Asset management

Which aspect of asset management does Adobe Bridge help streamline?

a) Cloud storage

b) Software development

c) Keyword tagging

d) Social media marketing

Answer: c) Keyword tagging

How does Adobe Bridge contribute to efficient collaboration within creative teams?

a) It offers video conferencing tools.

b) It provides project management features.

c) It centralizes and organizes media assets.

d) It automatically generates design concepts.

Answer: c) It centralizes and organizes media assets.

What role does Adobe Bridge play in relation to Chapter 15's focus on integration?

a) It helps manage team schedules.

b) It facilitates budget allocation.

c) It enables seamless asset integration with other Creative Cloud apps.

d) It automates project timelines.

Answer: c) It enables seamless asset integration with other Creative Cloud apps.

Which feature of Adobe Bridge allows users to view images, videos, and documents without opening separate applications?

a) Batch processing

b) Asset synchronization

c) Visual previews

d) Cloud-based storage

Answer: c) Visual previews

How does Adobe Bridge enhance consistency in asset organization?

a) It applies automatic color corrections to images.

b) It connects to social media platforms for content distribution.

c) It provides real-time collaboration tools.

d) It allows users to assign metadata and keywords to assets.

Answer: d) It allows users to assign metadata and keywords to assets.

What advantage does Adobe Bridge's batch renaming feature offer to creative professionals?

a) It converts files between different formats.

b) It enables automatic watermarking of images.

c) It enhances the resolution of images.

d) It saves time when renaming multiple files simultaneously.

Answer: d) It saves time when renaming multiple files simultaneously.

How does Adobe Bridge's integration with Creative Cloud apps impact workflow efficiency?

a) It replaces the need for Creative Cloud subscriptions.

b) It automates content creation.

c) It allows users to manage assets independently of other applications.

d) It enables seamless transition between asset management and content creation.

Answer: d) It enables seamless transition between asset management and content creation.

Which benefit does Adobe Bridge's Adobe Stock integration provide to users?

a) Automatic cloud backup for assets

b) Access to premium Adobe fonts

c) Direct access to Adobe customer support

d) Convenient access to licensed assets for use in projects

Answer: d) Convenient access to licensed assets for use in projects

What type of assets can be managed and organized using Adobe Bridge?

a) Only images

b) Only video files

c) Images, videos, audio files, and documents

d) Only vector graphics

Answer: c) Images, videos, audio files, and documents

Chapter 16: Exporting and Publishing

Export settings for print, web, and multimedia

1. Export Settings for Print:

Exporting content for print requires careful consideration of color modes, resolution, and file formats to ensure high-quality output on physical mediums like paper or other printable materials. Here are some key points to keep in mind:

Color Mode: Print materials are often produced in the CMYK color mode, which is optimized for four-color printing (Cyan, Magenta, Yellow, and Black). Be sure to convert your design to CMYK to ensure accurate color reproduction.

Resolution: Print requires higher resolution than digital formats. A common rule of thumb is to use a resolution of 300 DPI (dots per inch) to ensure crisp and detailed images.

File Format: The standard file formats for print include PDF (Portable Document Format) and TIFF (Tagged Image File Format). PDF is widely used for documents containing both images and text, as it maintains the layout and can embed fonts. TIFF is suitable for high-resolution images without loss of quality.

Bleed and Crop Marks: If your design extends to the edge of the page, it's essential to include a bleed area (extra space beyond the final trim size) to account for slight variations during printing. Crop marks indicate where the paper should be trimmed after printing.

2. Export Settings for Web:

When preparing content for the web, the focus shifts to optimizing for screen display, fast loading times, and compatibility across different devices and browsers. Here's what you should consider:

Color Mode: Web content is typically created in the RGB color mode, as screens emit color using red, green, and blue light. Keep your design in RGB for vibrant on-screen visuals.

Resolution: Screens have a lower resolution compared to print, usually 72 DPI. Higher resolutions might not result in better quality and will unnecessarily increase file sizes.

File Format: For images with transparency, use PNG format. For photographs and complex images, JPEG is suitable due to its smaller file size. For graphics with limited colors and sharp edges, consider using GIF. SVG (Scalable Vector Graphics) is great for logos and icons, as they can be scaled without loss of quality.

Compression: Use appropriate compression techniques to balance image quality and file size. Tools like image optimizers or exporting options in graphic software can help achieve this.

3. Export Settings for Multimedia:

Multimedia projects involve various elements, such as images, videos, audio, and animations. Exporting settings for multimedia projects depend on the specific medium and platform you're targeting:

Video: When exporting videos for multimedia projects, consider the target platform and the desired quality. Common video formats include MP4 (H.264 codec) for web and streaming platforms. Adjust the resolution and bitrate based on the platform's recommendations.

Audio: For audio elements, formats like MP3 or AAC are widely supported. Choose the appropriate bitrate to balance audio quality and file size.

Animations: For animations, formats like GIF, APNG (Animated PNG), or even HTML5 animations can be used. Consider compatibility with the target devices and browsers.

Interactive Multimedia: For interactive multimedia projects, consider the platform you're building for (e.g., mobile app, web application). Export assets and interactive components in formats compatible with the development environment.

In conclusion, Chapter 16: Exporting and Publishing focuses on the critical phase of preparing your content for different platforms. By understanding the specific requirements of print, web, and multimedia, you can ensure that your creations are presented optimally, whether they're in the form of printed materials, web pages, or multimedia experiences. Always tailor your export settings to the medium, keeping in mind factors such as color modes, resolution, file formats, and compatibility to achieve the best results.

QUIZ

Question 1: What is the recommended color mode for print materials?

a) RGB

b) HSV

c) CMYK

d) Pantone

Answer: c) CMYK

Question 2: What is the standard resolution for print images to ensure high quality?

a) 72 DPI

b) 150 DPI

c) 300 DPI

d) 600 DPI

Answer: c) 300 DPI

Question 3: Which file format is commonly used for print documents that contain both images and text?

a) PNG

b) TIFF

c) GIF

d) SVG

Answer: b) TIFF

Question 4: Which color mode is suitable for web content to ensure vibrant on-screen visuals?

a) RGB

b) CMYK

c) Pantone

d) HEX

Answer: a) RGB

Question 5: What is the purpose of a bleed area in print design?

a) To mark the area where the paper should be trimmed.

b) To indicate the safe zone for text and important elements.

c) To add extra space for variations during printing.

d) To optimize images for web display.

Answer: c) To add extra space for variations during printing.

Question 6: Which image format is best for graphics with limited colors and sharp edges?

a) JPEG

b) PNG

c) GIF

d) TIFF

Answer: c) GIF

Question 7: Which video format is commonly used for web and streaming platforms?

a) AVI

b) MP4

c) WMV

d) MOV

Answer: b) MP4

Question 8: What is the primary consideration when exporting audio for multimedia projects?

a) Bitrate

b) Color mode

c) Resolution

d) Compression

Answer: a) Bitrate

Question 9: What format is suitable for scalable vector graphics that maintain quality when resized?

a) PNG

b) JPEG

c) GIF

d) SVG

Answer: d) SVG

Question 10: Which multimedia format is used for animations that support transparency and simple interactivity?

a) MP4

b) AVI

c) GIF

d) MP3

Answer: c) GIF

Publishing to various formats and platforms

1. Print Publishing:

When preparing content for print, you need to ensure that your materials are properly formatted for physical distribution. Here's how you can approach print publishing:

Layout and Formatting: Arrange your content in a visually pleasing and organized manner, considering factors such as page margins, font sizes, and alignment.

Typography: Choose appropriate fonts that are easy to read in print. Ensure consistent typography throughout the document.

Images: Ensure that images are of high resolution and CMYK color mode to maintain print quality. Position images within the layout and consider captions or labels if necessary.

Color Consistency: Make sure the colors in your design match the intended output by using color profiles and calibration tools.

Bleed and Trim Marks: If your design extends to the edge of the page, include bleed areas and crop marks to ensure proper trimming during printing.

File Format: Export your print-ready materials in formats like PDF or TIFF that preserve layout and quality.

2. Web Publishing:

Web publishing involves optimizing your content for online platforms, considering factors like screen size, responsiveness, and user experience:

Responsive Design: Create a design that adapts to various screen sizes, ensuring a consistent and user-friendly experience on desktops, tablets, and smartphones.

Image Optimization: Compress images to balance quality and loading speed. Use appropriate image formats (JPEG, PNG, GIF) based on the content.

Web Typography: Choose web-safe fonts and ensure readability on screens. Use CSS to style fonts and maintain consistency.

Hyperlinks and Navigation: Ensure that links are functional and that navigation is intuitive. Utilize menus and buttons for easy access to different sections.

File Compression: Compress CSS, JavaScript, and other code files to improve website performance and loading times.

SEO Considerations: Add meta tags, relevant keywords, and descriptive alt text for images to improve search engine visibility.

File Formats: Publish web content using HTML, CSS, and JavaScript. Images can be in formats like JPEG, PNG, or SVG.

3. Multimedia Publishing:

For multimedia projects involving videos, animations, and audio, it's important to optimize for compatibility and quality:

Video Formats: Choose suitable video formats like MP4 (H.264 codec) for web and streaming platforms. Adjust resolutions and bitrates according to platform recommendations.

Audio Formats: Opt for widely supported audio formats like MP3 or AAC. Consider bitrates based on audio quality and file size requirements.

Animations: Export animations to formats like GIF or APNG for simple interactivity and transparency. Use HTML5 or other technologies for more complex animations.

Interactive Content: For multimedia projects with interactive elements, export assets and interactive components in formats compatible with the chosen development environment (e.g., HTML5, Unity).

4. Cross-Platform Publishing:

Sometimes, you might need to publish content across multiple platforms. In this case:

Content Adaptation: Customize your content to suit the strengths and limitations of each platform while maintaining a consistent brand identity.

Asset Management: Organize and manage assets (images, videos, fonts) effectively to streamline publishing across different platforms.

Testing: Test your content on different devices and browsers to ensure consistent rendering and functionality.

In conclusion, Chapter 16: Exporting and Publishing addresses the crucial step of making your content available to your audience. By understanding the unique requirements and characteristics of print, web, multimedia, and other platforms, you can effectively prepare and publish your work while maintaining quality and accessibility across various mediums. Always tailor your approach to the specific platform, considering aspects like layout, formatting, typography, images, and interactivity to create a successful and engaging final product.

QUIZ

Question 1: Which format is commonly used for print publishing to preserve layout and quality?

a) JPEG

b) PDF

c) PNG

d) GIF

Answer: b) PDF

Question 2: What is responsive design in the context of web publishing?

a) Designing for various print sizes

b) Designing for different content types

c) Designing for different screen sizes and devices

d) Designing for search engine optimization

Answer: c) Designing for different screen sizes and devices

Question 3: When optimizing images for web publishing, what is the main consideration?

a) Resolution

b) Color mode

c) File format

d) Typeface

Answer: c) File format

Question 4: Which image format is suitable for graphics with transparency and support for animations?

a) JPEG

b) PNG

c) GIF

d) TIFF

Answer: c) GIF

Question 5: What should be considered when publishing multimedia projects with interactive elements?

a) Use only GIF animations

b) Optimize for print resolution

c) Export assets compatible with the development environment

d) Use CMYK color mode

Answer: c) Export assets compatible with the development environment

Question 6: Which step is important when preparing content for cross-platform publishing?

a) Use the same layout and assets for all platforms

b) Customize content for each platform's strengths and limitations

c) Ignore compatibility testing on different devices

d) Use high-resolution images regardless of platform requirements

Answer: b) Customize content for each platform's strengths and limitations

Question 7: What is the primary purpose of including bleed areas and crop marks in print designs?

a) To add decorative elements to the design

b) To indicate where text should be placed

c) To mark the area for printer calibration

d) To account for slight variations during printing and trimming

Answer: d) To account for slight variations during printing and trimming

Question 8: When choosing fonts for web publishing, what should be considered?

a) Use a single font throughout the website for consistency

b) Choose fonts that look good in print

c) Use decorative fonts to make the website stand out

d) Choose web-safe fonts that are easily accessible to users

Answer: d) Choose web-safe fonts that are easily accessible to users

Question 9: Which multimedia format is commonly used for videos on web and streaming platforms?

a) AVI

b) MP4

c) WMV

d) MOV

Answer: b) MP4

Question 10: What is the purpose of adding relevant keywords and meta tags in web publishing?

a) Enhance the visual appeal of the website

b) Increase loading speed

c) Improve search engine visibility

d) Provide copyright information

Answer: c) Improve search engine visibility

Chapter 17: Mobile Creativity with Adobe Apps

Overview of Adobe's mobile app offerings

Adobe Photoshop Express:

Adobe Photoshop Express is a simplified version of the renowned desktop software, Photoshop. It offers essential photo editing tools such as cropping, rotating, resizing, exposure adjustments, filters, and basic retouching. This app is suitable for quick edits and enhancements to your photos.

Adobe Lightroom:

Adobe Lightroom is a powerful photo editing and organizing app tailored for mobile devices. It allows users to edit raw photos, apply presets, adjust lighting, color balance, and manage their photo library effectively. Lightroom's non-destructive editing ensures that the original image remains untouched.

Adobe Illustrator Draw:

Illustrator Draw is a vector-based drawing app that lets users create intricate illustrations with precision. It offers a variety of brushes, shapes, and tools to facilitate detailed designs.

The vector format ensures that the artwork can be scaled without losing quality.

Adobe Fresco:

Adobe Fresco combines raster and vector tools, making it an ideal app for digital artists and illustrators. It offers a wide range of brushes that mimic natural media like oils, watercolors, and pencils. The app's Live Brushes even simulate the behavior of real watercolors.

Adobe Spark:

Adobe Spark encompasses three tools: Spark Post for graphic design, Spark Video for creating videos, and Spark Page for designing web pages. These apps are user-friendly and focus on creating visual content for social media, presentations, and simple web projects.

Adobe Premiere Rush:

Adobe Premiere Rush is a video editing app that enables users to create professional-quality videos right from their mobile devices. It offers features like multi-track editing, transitions, color correction, and the ability to sync projects across devices.

Adobe Aero:

Adobe Aero is an augmented reality (AR) authoring tool that allows users to create interactive AR experiences without needing coding skills. It's particularly useful for designers looking to integrate digital content into the real world.

Adobe Capture:

Adobe Capture lets users turn real-world elements into digital assets. With Capture, you can create color themes, patterns, brushes, and vector shapes by capturing them through your device's camera.

Adobe Scan:

Adobe Scan is a document scanning app that utilizes your device's camera to convert physical documents into editable digital files. This is valuable for users who need to digitize documents on the go.

Adobe XD:

Adobe XD is a user experience (UX) and user interface (UI) design app for creating interactive prototypes and designs. It's especially useful for web and app designers who want to visualize and test their ideas before implementation.

These Adobe mobile apps are designed to complement each other and can often integrate seamlessly with their desktop counterparts through Adobe Creative Cloud. This allows users to start projects on their mobile devices and continue working on them on their computers, providing a flexible and convenient workflow for creative professionals and enthusiasts alike. The mobile app offerings from Adobe provide a versatile toolkit for unleashing creativity in a mobile-first world.

QUIZ

Which Adobe mobile app is specifically designed for creating intricate vector illustrations on mobile devices?

a) Adobe Lightroom

b) Adobe Photoshop Express

c) Adobe Illustrator Draw

d) Adobe Spark

Answer: c) Adobe Illustrator Draw

Which Adobe mobile app offers a variety of brushes that simulate natural media like oils, watercolors, and pencils?

a) Adobe Fresco

b) Adobe Premiere Rush

c) Adobe Spark

d) Adobe Aero

Answer: a) Adobe Fresco

What is the primary purpose of Adobe Spark mobile app?

a) Video editing

b) Augmented reality authoring

c) Photo retouching

d) Graphic design, video creation, and web page design

Answer: d) Graphic design, video creation, and web page design

Which Adobe mobile app is suitable for creating interactive augmented reality experiences without coding skills?

a) Adobe Fresco

b) Adobe Aero

c) Adobe Capture

d) Adobe XD

Answer: b) Adobe Aero

Adobe Scan is primarily used for:

a) Creating digital illustrations

b) Editing videos

c) Scanning and digitizing physical documents

d) Designing web pages

Answer: c) Scanning and digitizing physical documents

Which Adobe mobile app allows users to create non-destructive edits to raw photos and manage their photo library?

a) Adobe Lightroom

b) Adobe Photoshop Express

c) Adobe Premiere Rush

d) Adobe Capture

Answer: a) Adobe Lightroom

Which Adobe mobile app is suitable for designing user interfaces and interactive prototypes for web and app projects?

a) Adobe Fresco

b) Adobe XD

c) Adobe Spark

d) Adobe Scan

Answer: b) Adobe XD

Adobe Illustrator Draw is primarily used for creating:

a) Video animations

b) Vector illustrations

c) Augmented reality experiences

d) Document scanning

Answer: b) Vector illustrations

Which Adobe mobile app offers a range of brushes that mimic natural media like oils, watercolors, and pencils?

a) Adobe Photoshop Express

b) Adobe Spark

c) Adobe Fresco

d) Adobe Capture

Answer: c) Adobe Fresco

Which Adobe mobile app is designed to help users capture real-world elements and turn them into digital assets like color themes, patterns, and brushes?

a) Adobe Lightroom

b) Adobe Spark

c) Adobe Capture

d) Adobe Premiere Rush

Answer: c) Adobe Capture

Creating on-the-go with tablets and smartphones

In the modern era, where mobile devices have become an integral part of our lives, they also play a crucial role in fostering creativity. Tablets and smartphones are no longer just communication devices; they have evolved into powerful tools that enable individuals to create art, design, and media content wherever they are. Adobe's suite of mobile apps takes full advantage of these devices' capabilities, making it possible for professionals and enthusiasts alike to produce high-quality creative work while on the move.

Benefits:

Portability and Convenience: Tablets and smartphones are compact and lightweight, allowing creatives to carry their workstations wherever they go. This level of portability ensures that inspiration can strike at any time and place, without being tied to a specific location.

Touchscreen Interaction: Touchscreens offer an intuitive way to interact with creative apps. With gestures like tapping, swiping, pinching, and rotating, users can manipulate designs, photos, and artwork with precision, simulating the experience of using traditional artistic tools.

Instant Capture: Mobile devices are equipped with high-resolution cameras that can capture photos, sketches, and visual references directly. This feature enables artists to gather inspiration from the real world and incorporate it into their work.

Real-Time Collaboration: Many Adobe mobile apps are designed for collaboration. Artists and designers can work on projects simultaneously, share drafts, and receive feedback in real-time, fostering teamwork even when team members are geographically dispersed.

Seamless Integration: Adobe's mobile apps often sync with their desktop counterparts through cloud services like Adobe Creative Cloud. This integration ensures that projects can be started on mobile devices and seamlessly continued on desktop computers, maintaining a consistent workflow.

Challenges:

Limited Screen Real Estate: The smaller screen size of mobile devices might pose challenges when working on complex projects that require extensive detail or a broad canvas.

Processing Power: While mobile devices have become more powerful, they might still lag behind desktop computers in terms of processing capabilities, which could affect the performance of resource-intensive applications.

Battery Life: Intensive creative work can drain the battery of mobile devices quickly. This limitation might require users to plan their creative sessions and ensure access to charging solutions.

Techniques and Tips:

Simplify your Workflow: When working on a mobile device, focus on the essential aspects of your project. Streamline your workflow to accommodate the device's limitations and leverage its strengths.

Use Styluses: If your device supports it, consider using a stylus for more precise input. This can enhance the accuracy and control you have over your creative process.

Utilize Cloud Storage: Save your work to the cloud regularly to prevent data loss. Cloud storage also facilitates easy access to your projects from various devices.

Experiment with Mobile-First Features: Adobe's mobile apps often have features that are tailor-made for touch interactions and mobile capabilities. Experiment with these features to discover new creative possibilities.

Stay Inspired: Use your device's camera to capture interesting textures, colors, and scenes from the world around you. These can serve as inspiration for your creative projects.

In conclusion, the chapter "Creating on-the-go with tablets and smartphones" within the book "Mobile Creativity with Adobe Apps" likely explores how these portable devices have transformed into creative powerhouses with the aid of Adobe's mobile apps. By understanding the benefits, challenges, techniques, and tips, users can harness the full potential of these devices to create impressive art, design, and media content, all while being untethered from traditional workstations.

QUIZ

What is a significant advantage of creating on-the-go with tablets and smartphones?

a) Larger screen size for detailed work

b) Limited portability

c) Incompatibility with creative apps

d) Ability to work from anywhere

Answer: d) Ability to work from anywhere

How can touchscreens enhance the creative process on mobile devices?

a) They can print physical copies of artwork.

b) They offer advanced coding capabilities.

c) They allow intuitive interaction with creative apps.

d) They enable voice recognition for design commands.

Answer: c) They allow intuitive interaction with creative apps.

What is a potential challenge when working on creative projects with mobile devices?

a) Excessive processing power

b) Unlimited battery life

c) Lack of cloud storage

d) Limited screen real estate

Answer: d) Limited screen real estate

How does cloud storage benefit creative work on mobile devices?

a) It enhances battery life.

b) It provides physical storage options.

c) It ensures data loss prevention and cross-device access.

d) It allows for offline editing only.

Answer: c) It ensures data loss prevention and cross-device access.

Which aspect of using styluses is beneficial for creative work on mobile devices?

a) Decreased accuracy

b) Limited compatibility

c) Enhanced precision and control

d) Increased battery consumption

Answer: c) Enhanced precision and control

What is one technique for adapting to the limitations of working on a mobile device?

a) Complicating the workflow to utilize device capabilities fully

b) Ignoring cloud storage to save processing power

c) Using only resource-intensive applications

d) Streamlining the workflow to accommodate device limitations

Answer: d) Streamlining the workflow to accommodate device limitations

What role does real-time collaboration play in creating on-the-go with mobile devices?

a) It increases battery consumption.

b) It restricts access to local networks only.

c) It hampers creativity due to conflicting opinions.

d) It fosters teamwork and allows simultaneous work on projects.

Answer: d) It fosters teamwork and allows simultaneous work on projects.

Which feature of Adobe's mobile apps ensures that projects can be started on mobile devices and continued on desktop computers?

a) Cloud storage limitations

b) Offline-only editing

c) Seamless integration with Adobe Creative Cloud

d) Incompatibility with touchscreens

Answer: c) Seamless integration with Adobe Creative Cloud

What is a common concern when working extensively on creative projects with mobile devices?

a) Excessive screen size

b) Frequent need for manual updates

c) Quick battery depletion

d) Lack of stylus support

Answer: c) Quick battery depletion

How can utilizing your device's camera contribute to your creative process?

a) It replaces the need for stylus input.

b) It can capture inspiration from the real world.

c) It improves the performance of resource-intensive apps.

d) It restricts your creative process to photography only.

Answer: b) It can capture inspiration from the real world.

Chapter 18: Tips for Efficient Workflow

Keyboard shortcuts and time-saving techniques

In today's fast-paced digital world, efficiency and productivity are key factors in maintaining a successful workflow. One of the most effective ways to enhance your efficiency is by mastering keyboard shortcuts and implementing time-saving techniques. This chapter explores the significance of keyboard shortcuts and offers valuable insights into how they can be integrated into your daily workflow for maximum productivity.

1. Understanding Keyboard Shortcuts:

Keyboard shortcuts are combinations of keys that perform specific actions within software applications, operating systems, or even web browsers. Instead of navigating through menus or using the mouse to access various functions, keyboard shortcuts allow you to execute tasks quickly and directly. They are designed to save time, reduce repetitive movements, and enhance overall productivity.

2. Benefits of Keyboard Shortcuts:

Time-Saving: Keyboard shortcuts eliminate the need to manually navigate through menus, leading to significantly faster task completion.

Reduced Strain: Relying less on the mouse can help reduce strain on your wrist and fingers, minimizing the risk of repetitive strain injuries.

Focused Workflow: Using shortcuts keeps your hands on the keyboard, allowing for a more focused and uninterrupted workflow.

Consistency: Keyboard shortcuts are consistent across applications and platforms, which means mastering a few key combinations can benefit you across a range of software.

Efficiency: With practice, using keyboard shortcuts becomes second nature, allowing you to work more efficiently and confidently.

3. Time-Saving Techniques:

Learn the Basics: Start by familiarizing yourself with common keyboard shortcuts such as Ctrl + C (Copy), Ctrl + V (Paste), Ctrl + Z (Undo), Ctrl + S (Save), and Ctrl + F (Find). These are essential shortcuts that work across many applications.

Customization: Some applications allow you to customize keyboard shortcuts according to your preferences. Take advantage of this feature to tailor shortcuts to your specific workflow.

Use Cheat Sheets: Keep a cheat sheet or reference guide handy until you've memorized the shortcuts you use most frequently.

Practice Regularly: Consistent practice is key to internalizing shortcuts. Set aside time to consciously use them until they become second nature.

Master Application-Specific Shortcuts: Different software applications have their own set of unique shortcuts. Invest time in learning these shortcuts for the tools you frequently use.

Multitasking Shortcuts: Learn shortcuts that aid in multitasking, such as Alt + Tab (switching between open applications) or Ctrl + Tab (switching between tabs in a browser).

Universal Shortcuts: There are some universal shortcuts that work in almost all contexts, like Ctrl + C (Copy), Ctrl + V (Paste), and Ctrl + X (Cut).

Windows vs. Mac Shortcuts: Be aware of platform-specific shortcuts. While many are similar, there are differences between Windows and macOS shortcuts.

Browser Shortcuts: Popular web browsers like Chrome, Firefox, and Safari offer shortcuts for navigating between tabs, searching, and refreshing pages.

Text Editing Shortcuts: If you frequently work with text documents, mastering shortcuts for selection, navigation, and formatting can significantly speed up your workflow.

IDE and Coding Shortcuts: Integrated Development Environments (IDEs) and coding editors often have extensive shortcuts for code navigation, debugging, and code generation.

4. Developing Efficient Habits:

Regular Review: Periodically review your shortcuts to ensure you haven't forgotten any and to discover new ones that might have been introduced in updates.

Stay Open to Learning: Be open to discovering new shortcuts. If you come across a new one that could benefit your workflow, make an effort to incorporate it.

Refinement: As your workflow evolves, refine your use of shortcuts. Some shortcuts may become less relevant, while new ones might become crucial.

Conclusion:

Keyboard shortcuts and time-saving techniques are invaluable tools for streamlining your workflow and maximizing productivity. By mastering common shortcuts and embracing platform-specific and application-specific commands, you can significantly reduce the time spent on routine tasks and enhance your overall efficiency. Remember that consistent practice and a willingness to adapt are essential for successfully integrating these techniques into your daily work routine.

QUIZ

Question 1:

Which of the following is a key benefit of using keyboard shortcuts in your workflow?

A) Increased strain on wrists and fingers.

B) Slower task completion.

C) Reduced repetitive movements.

D) Less focus on efficient workflow.

Answer: C) Reduced repetitive movements.

Question 2:

Keyboard shortcuts are designed to:

A) Slow down workflow.

B) Increase the use of the mouse.

C) Save time and enhance productivity.

D) Be inconsistent across applications.

Answer: C) Save time and enhance productivity.

Question 3:

Which of the following is NOT a common keyboard shortcut?

A) Ctrl + C (Copy)

B) Ctrl + Z (Undo)

C) Ctrl + P (Paste)

D) Ctrl + S (Save)

Answer: C) Ctrl + P (Paste)

Question 4:

What's the advantage of using universal keyboard shortcuts?

A) They work only on certain platforms.

B) They work across various software applications.

C) They are difficult to memorize.

D) They require customization for each app.

Answer: B) They work across various software applications.

Question 5:

Which keyboard shortcut allows you to switch between open applications on Windows?

A) Ctrl + Tab

B) Alt + Tab

C) Shift + Tab

D) Ctrl + Shift + Esc

Answer: B) Alt + Tab

Question 6:

For efficient coding, what type of shortcuts do Integrated Development Environments (IDEs) typically offer?

A) Cooking shortcuts

B) Navigation shortcuts

C) Gardening shortcuts

D) Painting shortcuts

Answer: B) Navigation shortcuts

Question 7:

Why is regular practice important when learning keyboard shortcuts?

A) It's unnecessary; shortcuts are easy to remember.

B) Practice helps to forget shortcuts more quickly.

C) Consistent practice helps to internalize shortcuts.

D) It's only important for beginners, not experienced users.

Answer: C) Consistent practice helps to internalize shortcuts.

Organizing projects for maximum productivity

Efficiently organizing projects is a critical aspect of maintaining productivity and achieving success in any endeavor. Chapter 18 delves into the strategies and techniques that can be employed to organize projects for maximum efficiency, ensuring that tasks are well-structured, easily manageable, and contribute to a streamlined workflow.

1. Understanding Project Organization:

Project organization involves creating a systematic structure for planning, executing, and completing tasks. It encompasses defining project goals, breaking them down into manageable tasks, allocating resources, setting timelines, and establishing a clear workflow.

2. Benefits of Effective Project Organization:

Clarity: A well-organized project provides a clear roadmap for all team members, reducing confusion and ensuring everyone understands their roles and responsibilities.

Efficiency: With tasks properly outlined and assigned, there's less room for duplicated efforts or tasks falling through the cracks.

Productivity: Effective organization prevents time wastage on trying to figure out what needs to be done next or searching for resources.

Adaptability: A structured organization allows for easier adjustments in case of unexpected changes or challenges during the project.

Progress Tracking: Organized projects enable better monitoring of progress, allowing for timely adjustments and interventions if necessary.

Communication: Clear organization facilitates efficient communication, ensuring that team members are on the same page regarding project goals and updates.

3. Steps to Organize Projects Efficiently:

Define Project Goals: Clearly outline the project's objectives, scope, and desired outcomes. Ensure everyone involved understands the project's purpose and what is expected.

Break Down Tasks: Divide the project into smaller, manageable tasks. This granularity helps prevent overwhelm and allows for more accurate time estimation.

Prioritize Tasks: Identify critical tasks that need to be completed first and prioritize them based on their importance and dependencies.

Create a Timeline: Set realistic deadlines for each task and the overall project. Creating a timeline helps manage expectations and ensures steady progress.

Allocate Resources: Assign team members to tasks according to their skills and availability. Allocate resources such as budget, equipment, and materials.

Use Project Management Tools: Utilize project management tools such as Trello, Asana, or Microsoft Project to create task lists, assign responsibilities, and track progress.

Establish Milestones: Break the project timeline into meaningful milestones. These checkpoints serve as progress indicators and motivate the team to stay on track.

Communication Plan: Develop a communication plan that outlines how team members will share updates, address challenges, and discuss project-related matters.

Document Everything: Keep detailed records of decisions, changes, and discussions. Documentation helps in maintaining accountability and provides a reference for future projects.

4. Tips for Effective Project Organization:

Keep It Simple: Avoid overcomplicating the organizational structure. Strive for simplicity to prevent confusion and unnecessary complexities.

Regular Review: Periodically review and adjust the project organization as needed. Projects may evolve, and staying adaptable is key.

Collaboration: Involve all relevant stakeholders In the project organization process to ensure alignment and buy-in from the entire team.

Centralize Resources: Store all project-related documents, files, and resources in a centralized location that is easily accessible to the team.

Delegate and Empower: Empower team members by delegating tasks and providing them with the autonomy to make decisions within their scope.

Celebrate Achievements: Celebrate milestones and achievements along the way. Recognizing progress boosts team morale and motivation.

Conclusion:

Effective project organization is a cornerstone of a productive workflow. By following a structured approach, breaking down tasks, creating timelines, and utilizing project management tools, individuals and teams can ensure that their projects are well-executed and efficiently managed from start to finish. An organized project not only saves time and resources but also contributes to a smoother and more successful work process.

QUIZ

Question 1:

What is the primary goal of organizing projects for maximum productivity?

A) Adding complexity to the project.

B) Slowing down the project timeline.

C) Reducing the need for communication.

D) Streamlining workflow and improving efficiency.

Answer: D) Streamlining workflow and improving efficiency.

Question 2:

Why is breaking down tasks an important step in project organization?

A) It makes the project more complex.

B) It reduces the need for communication.

C) It helps prevent team involvement.

D) It makes tasks more manageable and reduces overwhelm.

Answer: D) It makes tasks more manageable and reduces overwhelm.

Question 3:

What is the purpose of creating milestones in a project organization?

A) To add unnecessary tasks to the project.

B) To increase the overall project duration.

C) To motivate the team and track progress.

D) To make the project more confusing.

Answer: C) To motivate the team and track progress.

Question 4:

Which type of tool can be used to create task lists, assign responsibilities, and track progress in a project?

A) Projector

B) Spreadsheet

C) Notepad

D) Project management tool

Answer: D) Project management tool

Question 5:

Why is it important to allocate resources in project organization?

A) To make the project more complicated.

B) To discourage collaboration among team members.

C) To ensure the project stays within budget and is well-equipped.

D) To increase the number of tasks in the project.

Answer: C) To ensure the project stays within budget and is well-equipped.

Question 6:

What does an effective communication plan in project organization involve?

A) Keeping all communication within the project manager.

B) Avoiding any communication until the project is complete.

C) Outlining how team members will share updates and address challenges.

D) Only communicating with external stakeholders.

Answer: C) Outlining how team members will share updates and address challenges.

Question 7:

Why is it important to periodically review and adjust project organization?

A) It's not necessary; project organization remains constant.

B) To make the project more confusing for team members.

C) Projects never evolve, so review is not needed.

D) Projects may evolve, and adjustments ensure alignment with changing goals.

Answer: D) Projects may evolve, and adjustments ensure alignment with changing goals.

Chapter 19: Troubleshooting and Support

Common issues and their solutions

1. Slow Performance:

Issue: Systems, applications, or networks running slower than expected.

Possible Causes: Resource limitations, background processes, malware, outdated hardware or software.

Solutions: Clear temporary files, update software and drivers, upgrade hardware, close unnecessary background processes, run malware scans, optimize system settings.

2. Software Crashes:

Issue: Applications crashing or freezing unexpectedly.

Possible Causes: Software bugs, conflicts with other applications, insufficient system resources.

Solutions: Update the software, check for patches or hotfixes, disable conflicting plugins/extensions, increase available system resources, reinstall the application.

3. Connectivity Problems:

Issue: Inability to connect to the internet or network.

Possible Causes: Network configuration issues, hardware problems, incorrect settings.

Solutions: Check cables and connections, reset networking equipment, troubleshoot IP configurations, verify firewall settings, update network drivers.

4. Blue Screen of Death (BSOD):

Issue: Windows system displaying a blue screen with error codes.

Possible Causes: Hardware or driver conflicts, memory issues, system file corruption.

Solutions: Update drivers, perform memory tests, scan for malware, restore system files, check hardware compatibility.

5. Data Loss:

Issue: Accidental deletion or loss of important files.

Possible Causes: Human error, hardware failures, software corruption.

Solutions: Implement regular backups, use data recovery software, seek professional data recovery services.

6. Printer Issues:

Issue: Printing errors, paper jams, or inability to print.

Possible Causes: Incorrect printer settings, outdated drivers, hardware problems.

Solutions: Update printer drivers, check for paper jams, verify printer settings, restart print spooler service.

7. Security Breaches:

Issue: Unauthorized access, data breaches, malware infections.

Possible Causes: Weak passwords, unpatched systems, social engineering.

Solutions: Implement strong passwords, apply security updates, use antivirus/antimalware software, educate users about security best practices.

8. Application Compatibility:

Issue: Software not working as expected on a particular operating system or hardware.

Possible Causes: Incompatibility with OS version, missing dependencies.

Solutions: Check software compatibility requirements, use compatibility modes, install necessary libraries or components.

9. Email Problems:

Issue: Unable to send or receive emails, email client errors.

Possible Causes: Incorrect server settings, email account issues.

Solutions: Verify email server settings, check account credentials, troubleshoot email client configuration.

10. Battery Life Issues:

Issue: Rapid battery drain on laptops or mobile devices.

Possible Causes: Background processes, outdated software, battery wear.

Solutions: Close unused applications, update operating system, replace the battery if necessary, adjust power settings.

11. Unresponsive System:

Issue: System not responding to user input.

Possible Causes: Overloaded system resources, software conflicts, hardware failures.

Solutions: Restart the system, close unresponsive applications, diagnose hardware issues.

12. Application-Specific Problems:

Issue: Issues specific to certain software applications.

Possible Causes: Application bugs, outdated versions, corrupted files.

Solutions: Update the application, check for patches or updates, reinstall the application.

13. Network Performance Problems:

Issue: Slow network speeds or intermittent connectivity.

Possible Causes: Network congestion, router issues, ISP problems.

Solutions: Restart networking equipment, check for firmware updates, contact ISP if necessary.

14. Audio/Video Glitches:

Issue: Audio or video playback not smooth or distorted.

Possible Causes: Outdated drivers, hardware problems, codec issues.

Solutions: Update drivers, check hardware connections, use appropriate codecs.

In the Troubleshooting and Support chapter, the focus is on equipping users and professionals with the skills to diagnose and address these and other common issues. The solutions often involve a combination of technical knowledge, critical thinking, and effective communication to isolate and resolve problems efficiently. Moreover, promoting proactive practices such as regular maintenance, backups, and security measures can mitigate many of these issues before they become critical.

QUIZ

Question 1: What is a common cause of slow system performance?

A) High-speed internet connection

B) Excessive background processes

C) Running multiple applications simultaneously

D) Frequent system restarts

Answer: B) Excessive background processes

Question 2: Which action can help resolve software crashes in an application?

A) Reducing system RAM

B) Disabling firewall

C) Increasing background processes

D) Updating the application to the latest version

Answer: D) Updating the application to the latest version

Question 3: What can cause connectivity problems in a network?

A) Updating network drivers

B) Running network speed tests

C) Checking cables and connections

D) Installing more software applications

Answer: C) Checking cables and connections

Question 4: What does the "Blue Screen of Death" (BSOD) typically indicate?

A) Low battery warning

B) Network connectivity issue

C) Software conflict

D) System crash or error

Answer: D) System crash or error

Question 5: How can data loss be prevented effectively?

A) Avoiding system updates

B) Regularly performing data backups

C) Using a weak password

D) Leaving files on the desktop

Answer: B) Regularly performing data backups

Question 6: What could be a solution to printer issues such as paper jams?

A) Increasing print quality settings

B) Using incompatible ink cartridges

C) Checking for driver updates

D) Printing large files simultaneously

Answer: C) Checking for driver updates

Question 7: What is a common measure to enhance security and prevent unauthorized access?

A) Sharing passwords openly

B) Disabling all security software

C) Using strong and unique passwords

D) Ignoring software updates

Answer: C) Using strong and unique passwords

Accessing Adobe's support resources

Accessing Adobe's Support Resources

In Chapter 19: Troubleshooting and Support, one of the critical aspects is learning how to effectively access support resources provided by software companies, such as Adobe. Adobe is well-known for its wide range of creative software products like Photoshop, Illustrator, Acrobat, and more. When users encounter issues or need assistance with Adobe products, accessing Adobe's support resources becomes essential. Here's a detailed guide on how to do so:

1. Adobe Support Website:

Adobe's official support website is a comprehensive hub for troubleshooting and accessing resources. Follow these steps to access it:

Open your web browser and go to Adobe's official website (www.adobe.com).

Scroll to the bottom of the page and click on the "Support" link. This will direct you to Adobe's Support page.

On the Support page, you'll find various options to explore, including product-specific help, community forums, and contact options.

2. Product-Specific Troubleshooting:

Adobe offers product-specific troubleshooting guides and knowledge bases. Here's how to access them:

On the Adobe Support page, click on the "Products" tab or search for your specific Adobe product using the search bar.

Navigate to the product's support page, where you'll find links to troubleshooting guides, FAQs, and solutions to common problems.

3. Community Forums:

Adobe's community forums provide a platform for users to share experiences, ask questions, and collaborate on solutions. To access the forums:

On the Adobe Support page, click on the "Communities" tab or search for "Adobe [Product] Forum" on your preferred search engine.

Join the relevant product forum and post your query or search for existing threads that might address your issue.

4. Contacting Adobe Support:

If you're unable to resolve your issue through self-help resources, you can contact Adobe's support team. Here's how:

On the Adobe Support page, click on the "Contact Us" link.

You'll be presented with contact options such as live chat, phone support, and email support.

Choose the option that suits you best, and follow the prompts to get in touch with Adobe's support representatives.

5. Adobe Help Center:

Adobe offers a Help Center that covers a wide range of topics and products. To access it:

On the Adobe Support page, look for the "Help Center" link.

Browse through categories, such as "Getting Started," "Troubleshooting," and "Learn & Support," to find relevant information.

6. Social Media Channels:

Adobe often maintains active social media channels where they share updates, tips, and respond to user queries. You can follow Adobe on platforms like Twitter, Facebook, and Instagram for additional support resources.

7. Subscription Support:

If you're a subscriber to Adobe's Creative Cloud services, you might have access to priority support. Log in to your Adobe account and check for any premium support benefits included with your subscription.

In conclusion, accessing Adobe's support resources involves exploring the official support website, product-specific troubleshooting guides, community forums, and contacting their support team through various channels. Being familiar with these resources can significantly aid in efficiently resolving issues and getting the most out of Adobe's products.

QUIZ

Question 1: Where can users access Adobe's official support website?

A) www.adobe-support.com

B) www.adobe-helpdesk.com

C) www.adobe.com/support

D) www.adobe-troubleshoot.com

Answer: C) www.adobe.com/support

Question 2: What can users find in Adobe's product-specific troubleshooting guides?

A) Software activation keys

B) Product purchase options

C) Solutions to common problems

D) Personal user accounts

Answer: C) Solutions to common problems

Question 3: What is the primary purpose of Adobe's community forums?

A) To showcase Adobe's products

B) To offer free software downloads

C) To provide a platform for user collaboration

D) To advertise Adobe's support services

Answer: C) To provide a platform for user collaboration

Question 4: How can users contact Adobe's support team directly?

A) By visiting physical support centers

B) By sending letters via postal mail

C) Through live chat, phone, and email options

D) By posting on personal social media profiles

Answer: C) Through live chat, phone, and email options

Question 5: What can users find in Adobe's Help Center?

A) Entertainment news and celebrity gossip

B) A wide range of product manuals

C) Troubleshooting guides and resources

D) DIY home improvement projects

Answer: C) Troubleshooting guides and resources

Question 6: If you're an Adobe Creative Cloud subscriber, where might you find premium support options?

A) In your email inbox

B) In your software's preferences menu

C) In your Adobe account dashboard

D) In your computer's Control Panel

Answer: C) In your Adobe account dashboard

Question 7: How might following Adobe on social media platforms benefit users seeking support?

A) By providing free software downloads

B) By giving access to premium support services

C) By sharing updates, tips, and responding to queries

D) By granting direct access to Adobe's CEO

Answer: C) By sharing updates, tips, and responding to queries

Chapter 20: Beyond the Basics – Pushing Your Creativity

Exploring advanced techniques in selected applications

Chapter 20: Beyond the Basics – Pushing Your Creativity

Exploring Advanced Techniques in Selected Applications:

1. Art and Design:

In the realm of art and design, advanced techniques could include experimenting with different mediums, combining contrasting styles, or using cutting-edge digital tools to create intricate and interactive artworks. Artists might also explore techniques like surrealism, abstract expressionism, or hyperrealism to push the boundaries of traditional artistic approaches.

2. Writing and Literature:

In writing, advanced techniques might involve playing with narrative structure, using unreliable narrators, or experimenting with multiple points of view. Authors could explore nonlinear storytelling, intricate plot twists, or even incorporate multimedia elements to enhance the reading experience.

3. Film and Media Production:

In filmmaking, advanced techniques could include exploring new camera angles, using innovative editing styles, or experimenting with sound design to evoke specific emotions. Filmmakers might also push the boundaries of virtual reality or interactive storytelling, inviting the audience to become part of the narrative.

4. Music and Composition:

Musicians and composers could push their creativity by blending genres, experimenting with unconventional instruments, or incorporating technology like AI-generated music. Advanced techniques might involve complex time signatures, unique harmonies, or combining unexpected musical elements to create something truly original.

5. Problem Solving and Innovation:

Creativity isn't limited to the arts; it's essential in problem-solving and innovation too. Advanced techniques could involve design thinking, where one approaches challenges from multiple perspectives. Techniques like brainstorming, mind mapping, and TRIZ (Theory of Inventive Problem Solving) could be explored to find novel solutions.

6. Scientific Research:

In the realm of scientific research, pushing creativity involves thinking beyond conventional methodologies. Researchers might experiment with interdisciplinary collaborations, novel experimental designs, or harnessing the power of big data and machine learning to uncover new insights.

7. Cooking and Culinary Arts:

In the culinary world, advanced techniques could involve molecular gastronomy, combining unexpected flavors, or reimagining traditional dishes with a modern twist. Chefs might experiment with food presentation, textures, and even multisensory dining experiences.

8. Technology and Innovation:

Advancements in technology offer numerous opportunities for pushing creative boundaries. Augmented reality (AR), virtual reality (VR), and mixed reality (MR) can be employed to create immersive experiences. Innovators might also explore fields like AI-generated art, 3D printing, or even designing novel human-computer interfaces.

QUIZ

Question 1:

What is the primary focus of Chapter 20: "Beyond the Basics – Pushing Your Creativity"?

A) Exploring fundamental techniques in various applications.

B) Embracing conventional methods in creative endeavors.

C) Pushing creative boundaries using advanced techniques.

D) Discouraging experimentation in creative processes.

Answer: C) Pushing creative boundaries using advanced techniques.

Question 2:

In the field of art, an artist who combines contrasting styles and employs cutting-edge digital tools is likely:

A) Following traditional techniques.

B) Avoiding innovation.

C) Experimenting with advanced techniques.

D) Limiting creative expression.

Answer: C) Experimenting with advanced techniques.

Question 3:

Which domain involves techniques like nonlinear storytelling and experimenting with multiple points of view?

A) Cooking and Culinary Arts.

B) Problem Solving and Innovation.

C) Music and Composition.

D) Writing and Literature.

Answer: D) Writing and Literature.

Question 4:

In filmmaking, what could be considered an advanced technique to evoke specific emotions?

A) Sticking to conventional camera angles.

B) Employing simple editing techniques.

C) Using innovative camera angles and sound design.

D) Avoiding experimentation with sound.

Answer: C) Using innovative camera angles and sound design.

Question 5:

What does the concept of "design thinking" emphasize in problem-solving?

A) Sticking to one perspective.

B) Experimenting with unconventional approaches.

C) Avoiding collaboration with others.

D) Ignoring user feedback.

Answer: B) Experimenting with unconventional approaches.

Question 6:

Which field could involve pushing creative boundaries by experimenting with molecular gastronomy and reimagining traditional dishes?

A) Scientific Research.

B) Cooking and Culinary Arts.

C) Technology and Innovation.

D) Art and Design.

Answer: B) Cooking and Culinary Arts.

Question 7:

What is a key message conveyed by Chapter 20 in relation to creativity and innovation?

A) Creativity is limited to specific fields.

B) Innovation is unnecessary for creative growth.

C) Embrace change and experiment to push creativity.

D) Traditional methods are sufficient for creativity.

Answer: C) Embrace change and experiment to push creativity.

Integrating Adobe CC into your professional workflow

Integrating Adobe CC into Your Professional Workflow:

Adobe Creative Cloud is a suite of software applications and services that cover a wide range of creative disciplines such as graphic design, video editing, photography, web design, and more. Integrating Adobe CC into your professional workflow can significantly boost your creativity and productivity, allowing you to experiment with advanced techniques and innovative approaches.

1. Graphic Design and Illustration:

Adobe CC offers tools like Adobe Illustrator and Adobe Photoshop for graphic design and illustration. Advanced techniques include using vector graphics, experimenting with blend modes, and creating intricate designs using layers. Pushing your creativity involves exploring advanced features like 3D modeling, vector mesh manipulation, and combining various design elements.

2. Video Editing and Motion Graphics:

Adobe Premiere Pro and Adobe After Effects are widely used for video editing and motion graphics. To push your creativity, you can experiment with advanced video effects, keyframe animations, and color grading techniques. Integrating Adobe CC allows you to work seamlessly between these applications, enabling you to create visually stunning and engaging videos.

3. Photography and Image Manipulation:

Adobe Lightroom and Adobe Photoshop are essential for photographers and image manipulators. Pushing creativity in this context could involve advanced retouching techniques, HDR photography, and experimenting with composite images. Adobe CC's integration between Lightroom and Photoshop facilitates a smooth workflow for enhancing and transforming photographs.

4. Web Design and Development:

Adobe XD and Adobe Dreamweaver are tools for web design and development. You can push your creativity by designing interactive prototypes, experimenting with responsive design, and incorporating animations. Adobe CC's integration ensures you can seamlessly move from design to development, fostering a more efficient web creation process.

5. User Experience (UX) Design:

Adobe XD is a powerful tool for UX design. Integrating it into your workflow allows you to create interactive wireframes, prototypes, and user flows. Advanced techniques could involve creating complex interactions, testing user experiences, and collaborating with stakeholders to refine designs.

6. Publishing and Layout Design:

For publishing and layout design, Adobe InDesign is the go-to tool. To push your creativity, you can explore advanced typography, layout grids, and master pages. Adobe CC's integration facilitates the incorporation of multimedia elements and interactive features into your layouts.

7. Collaboration and Cloud Integration:

One of the strengths of Adobe CC is its cloud integration, which enables collaborative work across different projects. Pushing creativity involves using shared libraries, cloud storage, and collaboration tools to work seamlessly with team members, clients, and collaborators from various locations.

8. Animation and Character Design:

Adobe Animate is suitable for animation and character design. Pushing creativity might involve experimenting with frame-by-frame animations, creating interactive animations, and exploring advanced scripting for more complex interactions.

In conclusion, integrating Adobe Creative Cloud into your professional workflow aligns well with the theme of Chapter 20. By leveraging the advanced tools and features offered by Adobe CC, you can go beyond the basics and explore new techniques to enhance your creativity across various creative disciplines. Whether you're a graphic designer, photographer, videographer, or web developer, Adobe CC's versatility and integration empower you to push creative boundaries and bring innovative ideas to life.

QUIZ

Question 1:

What is the primary focus of Chapter 20: "Beyond the Basics – Pushing Your Creativity"?

A) Exploring fundamental techniques in various applications.

B) Promoting the use of conventional tools only.

C) Integrating Adobe CC into creative workflows.

D) Discouraging experimentation in creative processes.

Answer: C) Integrating Adobe CC into creative workflows.

Question 2:

Which Adobe CC tool is commonly used for graphic design and illustration?

A) Adobe Premiere Pro.

B) Adobe After Effects.

C) Adobe Illustrator.

D) Adobe Lightroom.

Answer: C) Adobe Illustrator.

Question 3:

What does integrating Adobe CC into your professional workflow enable you to do?

A) Limit creativity by using standard tools.

B) Access only basic design templates.

C) Push creative boundaries using advanced features.

D) Stick to traditional methods of creativity.

Answer: C) Push creative boundaries using advanced features.

Question 4:

Which Adobe CC application is ideal for creating interactive prototypes and user flows?

A) Adobe Photoshop.

B) Adobe InDesign.

C) Adobe XD.

D) Adobe Animate.

Answer: C) Adobe XD.

Question 5:

How can Adobe CC benefit collaboration in a professional workflow?

A) By restricting access to individual projects.

B) By limiting cloud integration options.

C) By facilitating shared libraries and collaboration tools.

D) By avoiding interactions with team members.

Answer: C) By facilitating shared libraries and collaboration tools.

Question 6:

Which Adobe CC tool is suitable for animation and character design?

A) Adobe Premiere Pro.

B) Adobe Illustrator.

C) Adobe After Effects.

D) Adobe Animate.

Answer: D) Adobe Animate.

Question 7:

What can pushing creativity with Adobe CC involve in the context of video editing?

A) Using standard transitions and effects.

B) Sticking to basic color correction techniques.

C) Experimenting with advanced video effects and animations.

D) Ignoring integration between Adobe CC applications.

Answer: C) Experimenting with advanced video effects and animations.

www.ingramcontent.com/pod-product-compliance
Lightning Source LLC
La Vergne TN
LVHW051431050326
832903LV00030BD/3032